AN OCCULT PHYSIOLOGY

AN
OCCULT
PHYSIOLOGY

RUDOLF   STEINER

Eight lectures given in Prague,
20th to 28th March, 1911

RUDOLF STEINER PRESS
LONDON

First Edition, 1932
Second Edition, revised 1951
Third Edition, revised 1983

Authorised translation from a shorthand report unrevised by the lecturer.

This English edition is published in agreement with the Rudolf Steiner Nachlass-verwaltung, Dornach, Switzerland. The original German text is published in the Complete Edition of the works of Rudolf Steiner entitled, *Eine okkulte Physiologie* (No 128 in the Bibliographical Survey 1961).

ISBN 85440 411 2 (paperback)

Printed and bound in Great Britain at
The Camelot Press Ltd, Southampton

British Library Cataloguing in Publication Data

Steiner, Rudolf
    An occult physiology.—3rd ed., rev.
    1. Human physiology
    I. Title   II. Eine okkulte Physiologie. *English*
    612   QP34.5

CONTENTS

ABOUT THE TRANSCRIPTS OF LECTURES

"The results of my anthroposophical work are, first, the books available to the general public; secondly, a great number of lecture-courses, originally regarded as private publications and sold only to members of the Theosophical (later Anthroposophical) Society. The courses consist of more or less accurate notes taken at my lectures, which for lack of time I have not been able to correct. I would have preferred the spoken word to remain the spoken word. But the members wished to have the courses printed for private circulation. Thus they came into existence. Had I been able to correct them the restriction: *for members only* would have been unnecessary from the beginning. As it is, the restriction was dropped more than a year ago.

In my autobiography it is especially necessary to say a word about how my books for the general public on the one hand, and the privately printed courses on the other, belong within what I elaborated as Anthroposophy.

Someone who wishes to trace my inner struggle and effort to present Anthroposophy in a way that is suitable for present-day consciousness must do so through the writings published for general distribution. In these I define my position in relation to the philosophical striving of the present. They contain what to my *spiritual sight* became ever more clearly defined, the edifice of Anthroposophy—certainly incomplete in many ways.

But another requirement arose, different from that of elaborating Anthroposophy and devoting myself solely to problems connected with imparting facts directly from the spiritual world to the general cultural life of today: the requirement of meeting fully the inner need and spiritual longing of the members.

Especially strong were the requests to have light thrown by Anthroposophy upon the Gospels and the Bible in general. The members wished to have courses of lectures on these revelations bestowed on mankind.

In meeting this need through private lecture courses, another factor arose: at these lectures only members were present. They were familiar with basic content of Anthroposophy. I could address them as people advanced in anthrophosophical knowledge. The approach I adopted in these lectures was not at all suitable for the written works intended primarily for the general public.

In these private circles I could formulate what I had to say in a way I should have been *obliged* to modify had it been planned initially for the general public.

Thus the public and the private publications are in fact two quite different things, built upon different foundations. The public writings are the direct result of my inner struggles and labours, whereas the privately printed material includes the inner struggle and labour of the members. I listened to the inner needs of the members, and my living experience of this determined the form of the lectures.

However, nothing was ever said that was not solely the result of my direct experience of the growing content of Anthrophosophy. There was never any question of concessions to the prejudices or the preferences of the members. Whoever reads these privately-printed lectures can take them to represent Anthroposophy in the fullest sense. Thus it was possible without hesitation—when the complaints in this direction became too persistent—to depart from the custom of circulating this material only among members. But it must be borne in mind that faulty passages occur in these lecture-reports not revised by myself.

The right to judge such private material can of course be conceded only to someone who has the pre-requisite basis for such judgment. And in respect of most of this material it would mean *at least* knowledge of man and of the cosmos insofar as these have been presented in the light of Anthroposophy, and also knowledge of what exists as 'anthroposophical history' in what has been imparted from the spiritual world."

Extract from *Rudolf Steiner, An Autobiography*, Chapter 35 pp. 386-388, 2nd Edition 1980, Steinerbooks, New York.

THE BEING OF MAN

Prague, 20th March, 1911.

This lecture-cycle deals with a subject which concerns Man very closely, namely, the exact nature and life of Man himself. Although so close to man, because it concerns himself, the subject is a difficult one to approach. For if we turn our attention to the challenge "Know thyself!", a challenge that has forced itself upon man through all the ages, as we may say, from mystic, occult heights, we see at once that a real, true self-knowledge is very hard of attainment. This applies not only to individual, personal self-knowledge, but above all to knowledge of the human being as such. Indeed it is precisely because man is so far from knowing his own being and has such a long way to go in order to know himself, that the subject we are about to discuss in the course of these few days will be in a certain respect something alien to us, something for which much preparation is necessary. Moreover it is not without reason that I myself have only reached the point where I can at last speak upon this theme as the result of mature reflection covering a long period of time. For it is a theme which cannot be approached with any prospect of arriving at a true and honest observation unless a certain attitude, often left out of account in ordinary scientific observation, be adopted. This attitude is one of reverence in the presence of the essential nature and *Being of Man*. It is, then, of vital importance that we maintain this attitude as a fundamental condition underlying the following reflections.

How can one truly maintain this reverence? In no other way, than by first disregarding what he appears to be in everyday life, whether it be oneself or another is of no consequence, and then by uplifting ourselves to the conception: Man, with all that he has evolved into, is not here for his own sake; he is here for the revelation of the Divine Spirit, of the whole World. He is a revelation of the Godhead of the World! And, when a man speaks of aspiring after self-knowledge, of aspiring to become ever more and more perfect, in the spiritual-scientific sense which has just been indicated, this should not be due to the fact that he desires merely from curiosity, or from a mere craving or knowledge, to know what man is; but rather that he feels it to be his duty to fashion ever more and more perfectly this representation, this revelation, of the World Spirit through Man, so that he may find some meaning in the words, "to remain unknowing is to sin against Divine destiny!" For the World Spirit has implanted in us the power to have knowledge; and, if we decline to develop knowledge, which we ought not to do, we thereby reject our task of becoming a revelation of the World Spirit. Instead of a revelation of the World Spirit we become a distorted image, a caricature of it. It is our duty to strive to become ever increasingly an image of the World Spirit. Only when we can give meaning to these words, "to become an image of the World Spirit"; only when it becomes significant for us in this sense to say, "We must learn to know, it is our duty to learn to know," only then can we sense aright that feeling of reverence we have just demanded, in the presence of the Being of Man. And for one who wishes to reflect, in the occult sense, upon the life of man, upon the essential quality of man's being, this reverence before the nature of man is an absolute necessity, for the simple reason that it is the only thing capable of awakening our spiritual sight, our entire spiritual faculty for seeing and beholding the things of the spirit, of awakening those forces which permit us to penetrate into the spiritual foundation of man's nature. Anyone who, as seer and investigator of the Spirit, is unable to have the very highest degree of reverence in the presence of the nature of man, who cannot permeate himself to the very fibres of his soul with the feeling of reverence before man's nature, must remain with closed eyes (however open they may be for this or that spiritual secret of the world) to all that concerns what is really deepest in the Being of Man. There may be many clairvoyants who can behold this or that in the spiritual environment of our existence; yet, if this reverence is lacking, they lack also the capacity to see into the depths of man's nature, and they will not know how to say anything rightly with regard to what constitutes the Being of Man.

In the external sense the teaching about life is called physiology. This teaching should not here be regarded in the same way as in external science but as it presents itself to the *spiritual eye*; so that we may look beyond the forms of the outer man, beyond the form and functions of his physical organs, of the life-forms and life processes. And as it is not our intention here to pursue this "occult physiology," in any amateurish way, it will be necessary to refer with complete candour to things which will sound rather improbable at first to anyone who is unfamiliar with these ideas. At the same time, it may be stated that this cycle of lectures, even more than some others I have delivered, forms a *whole,* and that no single part of any one lecture, especially the earlier ones—for much that is to find expression in the course of this cycle will have to be affirmed without restraint—should be torn from its context and judged separately. On the contrary, only after having heard the concluding lectures will it be possible to form a judgment with regard to what really has been said. For this reason, therefore, it will be necessary to proceed in a somewhat different way, in this occult physiology, from that of external physiology. The foundations for our introductory statements will be confirmed by what meets us at the conclusion. We shall not be called upon to draw a straight line, as it were, from the beginning to the end; but we shall proceed in a circle so that we shall return again, at the end, to the point from which we started.

It is an examination, a study, of Man, that is to be presented here. At first he appears before our external senses in his outer form. We know, of course, that to what in the first place the layman with his purely external observation can know concerning man, there is to-day a very great deal which science has added through research. Therefore, when considering what we are able to know at the present time about man's physical body through external experience and observation, we must of necessity combine what the layman is in a position to observe in himself and others with what science has to say, including those branches of scientific observation which come to their results through methods and instruments worthy of our admiration.

If we bear in mind first, purely as regards external man, all that a layman may observe in him (or may perhaps have learned from some sort of popular description of the nature of man), then it will perhaps not seem incomprehensible if, from the very beginning, attention is called to the fact that even the outer shape of man, as it meets us in the outside world, really consists of a duality. And for anyone who wishes to penetrate into the depths of human nature, it is absolutely necessary that he becomes conscious of the fact, that even external man, as regards his form and stature, presents fundamentally a duality.

One part of man, which we can clearly distinguish, consists of everything that is to be found enclosed in organs affording the greatest protection against the outside world: that is, all that we may include within the region of the *brain* and the *spinal cord*. Everything belonging in this connection to the nature of man, to the brain and spinal cord, is firmly enclosed in a secure protective bony structure. Taking a side view, we

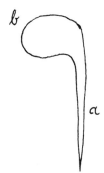

observe that what belongs to these two systems may be illustrated in the following way. If *a* in this diagram represents all the superimposed vertebrae along the whole length of the spinal cord, and *b* the cranium and the bones of the skull, then inside the canal which is formed by these superimposed vertebrae, as well as by the bones of the skull, is enclosed everything belonging to the sphere of the brain and the spinal cord. One cannot observe the human being without becoming conscious of the fact that everything pertaining to this region forms a totality complete within itself; and that the rest of man (which we might group physiologically in the most varied ways, as the neck, the trunk, the limb-structure) keeps its connection with all that we reckon as brain and spinal cord by means of more or less thread-like or ribbon-shaped formations, pictorially speaking, which must first break through this protective sheath, in order that a connection may be brought about between the portion enclosed within this bony structure and the portion attached to it as exterior nature of man. Thus we may say that, even to a superficial observation, everything constituting man proves itself to be a duality, the one portion lying within the bony structure we have described, the firm and secure protective sheath, and the other portion without.

At this point we must cast a purely superficial glance at that which lies within this bony structure. Here again we can quite easily distinguish between the large mass embedded within the skull-bones in the form of a brain, and that other portion which is appended to it like a stalk or cord and which, while organically connected with the brain, extends in this thread-like outgrowth of the brain into the spinal canal. If we differentiate between these two structures we must at once call attention to something which external science does not need to consider, something of which occult science, however, since its task is to penetrate into the depths of the being of things, must indeed take note. We must call attention to the fact that everything which we consider as the basis of a study of man refers, in the first place, only to Man. For the moment we enter into the profounder depths of the individual organs, we become aware (and we shall see in the course of these lectures that this is true) that any one of these organs, through its deeper significance in the case of man, may have an entirely different task from that of the corresponding organ in the animal world. Or, to put it more exactly, anyone who looks upon such things with the help of ordinary external science will say: "What you have been telling us here may be just as truly affirmed with reference to the animals." That which is said here, however, with reference to the essential nature of the organs in the case of the human being, cannot be said in the same way with regard to the animal. On the contrary the occult task is to consider the animal by itself, and to investigate whether that which we are in a position to state regarding man with reference to the spine and the brain, is valid also for animals. For the fact that the animals closely related to man also have a spinal cord and a brain does not prove that these organs, in their deeper significance, have the same task in both man and animal; just as the fact that a man holds a knife in his hand does not indicate whether it is for the purpose of carving a piece of veal or in order to erase something. In both cases we have to do with a knife; and he who considers only the form of the knife, that is, the knife as knife, will believe that in both cases it amounts to the same thing. In both cases, he who stands on the basis of a science that is not occult will say that we have to do with a spinal cord and a brain; and he will believe, since the same organs are to be found in man and animal, that these organs must therefore have the same function. But this is not true. It is something that has become a habit of thought in external science, and has led to certain inaccuracies; and it can be corrected only if external science will accustom itself gradually to enter into what can be stated from out of the depths of supersensible research regarding the different living beings.

Now, when we consider the spinal cord on the one hand, and the brain on the other, we can easily see that there is a certain element of truth in something already pointed out more than a hundred years ago by thoughtful students of nature. There is a certain rightness in the statement that when one observes the brain carefully it looks, so to speak, like a transformed spinal cord. This becomes all the more intelligible when we remember that Goethe, Oken, and other similarly reflective observers of nature, turned their attention primarily to the fact that the skull-bones bear certain resemblances of form to the vertebrae of the spine. Goethe, for example, was impressed very early in his reflections by the fact that when one imagines a single vertebra of the spinal column transformed, levelled and distended there may appear through such a reshaping of the vertebrae the bones of the head, the skull-bones; thus, if one should take a single vertebra and distend it on all sides so that it has elevations here and there, and at the same time is smooth and uniform in its expansions, the form of the skull might in this way be gradually derived from a single vertebra. Thus we may in a certain respect call the skull-bones reshaped vertebrae.

Now, just as we can look upon the skull-bones which enclose the brain as transformed vertebrae, as the transformation of such bones as enclose the spinal cord, so we may also think of the mass of the spinal cord distended in a different way, differentiated, more complex, till we obtain out of the spinal cord, so to speak, through this alteration, the brain. We might likewise, for instance, think how out of a plant, which at first has only green foliage, there grows forth the blossom. And so we might imagine that through the reshaping of a spinal cord, through its elevation to higher stages, the entire brain could be formed. (Later on, it will become clear how this matter is to be considered scientifically.) We may accordingly imagine our brain as a differentiated spinal cord.

Let us now look at both of these organs from this stand-point. Which of the two must we naturally look upon as the younger? Certainly not that one which shows the derived form, but rather the one which shows the original form. The spinal cord is at the first stage, it is younger; and the brain is at the second stage, it has gone through the stage of a spinal cord, is a transformed spinal cord, and is therefore to be considered as the older organ. In other words, if we fix our attention upon this new duality which meets us in man as brain and spinal cord, we may say that all the latent tend-encies, all the forces, which lead to the building of a brain must be older forces in man; for they must first, at an earlier stage, have formed the tendency to a spinal cord, and must then have worked further toward the re-forming of this beginning of a spinal cord into a brain. A second start, as it were, must therefore have been made, in which our spinal cord did not progress far enough to reach the second stage but remained at the stage of the spinal cord. Accordingly, in this spinal cord and nervous system if we wish to express ourselves with pedantic exactness we have a spinal cord of the *first* order; and in our brain a spinal cord of the *second* order, a re-formed spinal cord which has become older—a spinal cord which once was there as such, but which has been transformed into a brain.

Thus we have, in the first place, shown with absolute accuracy just what we need to consider when we fix our attention objectively upon the organic mass enclosed within this protective bony sheath. Here, however, something else must be taken into account, namely, something which really can confront us only in the field of occultism. A question may suggest itself, when for instance we speak as we have just been doing about the brain and the spinal cord, taking perhaps the following form: when such a re-formation as this takes place, from the plan of an organ at a first stage to the plan of an organ at a second stage, the evolutionary process may be progressive, or it may be retrogressive. That is, the process before us may either be one which leads to higher stages of perfection of the organ, or one which causes the organ to degenerate and gradually to die. We might say therefore, when we consider an organ like our spinal cord as it is to-day, that it seems to us to be at the present time a relatively young organ since it has not yet succeeded in becoming a brain. We may think about this spinal cord in two different ways. First, we may consider that it has in itself the forces through which it may also one day become a brain. In that case, it would be in a position to pass through a progressive evolution, and to become what our brain is to-day; or secondly, we may consider that it has not at all the latent tendency to attain to this second stage. In that case its evolution would be leading toward extinction; it would pass into decadence and be destined to suggest the first stage and not to arrive at the second. Now, if we reflect that the groundwork of our present brain is what was once the plan or beginning of a spinal cord, we see that that former spinal cord undoubtedly had in it the forces of a progressive evolution, since it actually did become a brain. If, on the other hand, we consider at this point our present spinal cord, the occult method of observation reveals that what to-day is our spinal cord has *not* within itself, as a matter of fact, the latent tendency to a forward-directed evolution, but is rather preparing to conclude its evolution at this present stage.

If I may express myself grotesquely, the human being is not called upon to believe that one day his spinal cord, which now has the form of a slender ribbon, will be puffed out as the brain is puffed out. We shall see later what underlies the occult view, so as to enable us to say this. Yet, through this simple comparison of the form of this organ in man and in the lower animals, where it first appears, you will find an external intimation of what has just been stated. In the snake, for example, the spine adds on to itself a series of innumerable rings behind the head and is filled out with the spinal cord, and this spinal column extends both forward and backward indefinitely. In the case of man the spinal cord, as it extends downward from the point where it is joined to the brain, actually tends more and more to a conclusion, showing less and less clearly that formation which it exhibits in its upper portions. Thus, even through external observation, one may notice that what in the case of the snake continues its natural evolution rearward, is here hastening toward a conclusion, toward a sort of degeneration. This is a method of observation through external comparison, and we shall see how the occult view affects it.

To summarise, then, we may say that within the bony structure of the skull we have a spinal cord which through a progressive development has become a brain, and is now at a second stage of its evolution; and in our spinal cord we have, as it were, the attempt once again to form such a brain, an attempt, however, which is destined to fail and cannot reach its full growth into a real brain.

Let us now proceed from this reflection to that which can be known even from an external, layman's observation, to the functions of the brain and the spinal cord. It is more or less known to everyone that the instrument of the so-called higher soul-activities, is in a certain respect, in the brain, that these higher soul-activities are directed by the organs of the brain. Furthermore, it is recognised that the more unconscious soul-activities are directed from the spinal cord. I mean those soul-activities in which very little deliberation interposes itself between the reception of the external impression and the action which follows it. Consider for a moment how you jerk back your hand when it is stung. Not very much deliberation intervenes between the sting and the drawing back. Such soul-activities as these are in fact, and with a certain justification, even regarded by natural science in such a way as to attribute to them the spinal cord as their instrument.

We have other soul-activities in which a more mature reflection interposes itself between the external impression and that which finally leads to action. Take, for example, an artist who observes external nature, straining every sense and gathering countless impressions. A long time passes, during which he works over these impressions in an inner activity of soul. He then proceeds to establish after a long interval through outward action what has grown, in long-continued soul-activity, out of the external impressions. Here there intervenes, between the outer impression and that which the man produces as a result of the outer impression, a richer activity of soul. This is also true of the scientific investigator; and, indeed, of anyone who reflects about the things that he wishes to do, and does not rush wildly at every external impression, who does not as it were, in reflex action fly into a passion like a bull when he sees the colour red, but thinks about what he wishes to do. In every instance where reflection intervenes, we encounter the brain as an instrument of soul-activity.

If we go still deeper into this matter we may say to ourselves: True, but how then does this soul-activity of ours, in which we use the brain, manifest itself? We perceive, to begin with, that it is of two different kinds, one of which takes place in our ordinary waking day-consciousness. In this consciousness we accumulate, through the senses, external impressions; and these we work over by means of the brain in rational reflection. To express it in popular language—we shall have to go into this still more accurately—we must picture to ourselves that these outer impressions find their way inside us through the doors of the senses, and stimulate certain processes in the brain. If we should wish, purely in connection with the external organisation, to follow what there takes place, we should see that the brain is set into activity through the stream of external impressions flowing into it; and that what this stream becomes, as a result of reflection, that is the deeds, the actions, which we ascribe to the instrumentality of the spinal cord.

Then, there also mingles in human life as it is to-day, between the wide-awake life of day and the unconscious life of sleep, the picture-life of dreams. This dream-life is a remarkable intermingling of the wide-awake life of day, which lays full claim to the instrument of our brain, and the unconscious life of sleep. Merely in outline, in a way that the lay thinker may observe for himself, we will now say something about this life of dreams.

We see that the whole of the dream-life has a strange similarity, from one aspect, to that subordinate soul-activity which we associate with the spinal cord. For, when dream-pictures emerge in our soul they do not appear as representations resulting from reflection, but rather by reason of a certain necessity, as, for instance, a movement of the hand results when a fly settles on the eye. In this latter case an action takes place as an immediate, necessary movement of defence. In dream-life something different appears, yet likewise because of an immediate necessity. It is not an action which here appears but rather a *picture* upon the horizon of the soul. Yet, just as we have no deliberate influence upon the movement of the hand in the wide-awake life of day, but make this movement of necessity, even so do we have no influence over the way that dream-pictures shape themselves, as they come and go in the chaotic world of dreams. We might say, therefore, that if we look at a man during his *wide-awake* life of day, and see something of what goes on within him in the form of reflex movements of all sorts, when he does things without reflecting, in response to external impressions; if we observe the sum-total of gestures and physiognomic expressions which he accomplishes without reflection, we then have a sum of actions which through necessity become a part of this man as soul-actions. If we now consider a *dreaming* man we have a sum of pictures, in this case something possessing the character not of action but of pictures, which work into and act upon his being. We may say, therefore, that just as in the wakeful life of day those human actions are carried out which arise and take shape without reflection, so do the dream-images, chaotically flowing together, come about within a world of pictures.

Now, if we look back again at our brain, and wished to consider it as being in a certain way the instrument also of the dream-consciousness, what should we have to do? We should have to suppose that there is in some way or other something inside the brain which behaves in a way similar to the spinal cord that guides the unconscious actions. Thus, we have, as it were, to look upon the brain as primarily the instrument of the wide-awake soul-life, during which we create our ideas through deliberation, and underlying it a mysterious spinal cord which does not express itself, however, as a complete spinal cord but remains compressed inside the brain, and does not attain to actions. Whereas our spinal cord does attain to *actions,* even though these are not brought about through deliberation; the brain in this case induces merely pictures. It stops midway, this mysterious thing which lies there like the groundwork of a brain. Might we not say, therefore, that the dream-world enables us in a most remarkable way to point, as in a mystery, to that spinal cord lying there at the basis of the brain?

If we consider the brain, in its present fully-developed state, as the instrument of our wide-awake life of day, its appearance for us is that which it has when removed from the cavity of the  skull. Yet there must be something there, within, when the wakeful life of day is blotted out. And here occult observation shows us that there actually is, inside the brain, a mysterious spinal cord which is the instrument of the dream life. If we should wish to make a drawing of it, we could represent it in such a way that, within the brain which is connected with the world of ideas of the life of day, we should have an ancient mysterious spinal cord, invisible to external perception, in some

THE BEING OF MAN

way or other secreted inside it. I shall first state quite hypothetically that this spinal cord becomes active when man
sleeps and dreams, and is active at that time in a manner
characteristic of a spinal cord, namely, that it calls forth
its effects through necessity. But, because it is compressed
within the brain, it does not lead to actions, but only to
pictures and picture-actions; for in dreams we act, as we
know, only in pictures. So that because of this peculiar,
strange, chaotic life that we carry on in dreams, we should
have to point to the fact that underlying the brain, which we
quite properly consider to be the instrument of our wide-
awake life of day, is a mysterious organ which perhaps represents an earlier form of the brain—which has evolved itself
to its present state out of this earlier form—and that this
mysterious organ is active to-day only when the new form is
inactive. It then reveals what the brain once was. This ancient
spinal cord conjures up what is possible, considering the way
it is enclosed, and induces, not completed actions, but only
pictures.

Thus the observation of life leads us, of itself, to separate
the brain into two stages. The very fact that we dream in-
dicates that the brain has passed through a spinal cord stage
and has evolved to the wide-awake life of day. When, however,
this wakeful day-time life is stilled, the ancient organ again
exerts itself in the life of dreams. Thus we have first made
types out of what external observation of the world furnishes
us, which shows us that even observation of the soul-life adds
meaning to what a consideration of the outer form can give
us, namely, that the wide-awake life of day is related to
dream-life in the same way as the perfected brain at the second
stage of its evolution is related to its groundwork, to the
ancient spinal cord which is at the first stage of its evolution.
In a remarkable way, which we shall justify in the following

lectures, occult, clairvoyant vision can serve us as a basis for a comprehensive observation of human nature, as it expresses itself in those organs enclosed within the bony mass of the skull and vertebrae.

In this connection you already know, from spiritual-scientific observations, that man's visible body is only one part of the whole human being, and that in the moment the seer's eye is opened the physical body reveals itself as enclosed, embedded, in a supersensible organism, in what, roughly speaking, is called the "human aura." For the present this may be here affirmed as a fact, and later we shall return to it to see how far the statement is justified. This human aura, within which physical man is simply enclosed like a kernel, shows itself to the seer's eye as having different colours. At the same time, we must not imagine that we could ever make a picture of this aura, for the colours are in continual movement; and every picture of it, therefore, that we sketch with pigment can be only an approximate likeness, somewhat in the same way that it is impossible to portray lightning, since one would always end by painting it only as it is never possible to paint lightning, so is it even less possible to do this in the case of the aura, because of the added fact that the auric colours are in themselves extraordinary unstable and mobile. We cannot, therefore, express it otherwise than to say that at best we are representing it symbolically.

Now, these auric colours show themselves as differing very remarkably, depending upon the fundamental character of the whole human organism. And it is interesting to call attention to the auric picture which presents itself to the clairvoyant eye, if we imagine the cranium and the spine observed from the rear. There we find that the appearance of that portion of the aura belonging to this region is such that we can only describe the whole man as embedded in the aura.

Although we must remember that the auric colours are in a state of movement within the aura, yet it is evident that one of the colours is especially distinct, namely around the lower parts of the spine. We may call this greenish. And again we may mention another distinct colour, which does not in any other part of the body appear so beautiful as here, around the region of the brain; and this in its ground-tone is a sort of lilac-blue. You can get the best conception of the lilac-blue if you imagine the colour of the peach-blossom; yet even this is only approximate. Between this lilac-blue of the upper portion of the brain, and the green of the lower parts of the spine, we have other colour nuances surrounding the human being which are hard to describe, since they do not often appear among the ordinary colours present in the surrounding world of the senses. Thus, for instance, adjoining the green is a colour which is neither green, blue, nor yellow, but a mixture of all three. In short, there appear to us, in this intermediate space, colours which actually do not exist in the physical world of sense. Even though it is difficult to describe what is here within the aura, one thing may nevertheless be stated positively: beginning above with the puffed-out spinal cord, we have lilac-blue colour and then,

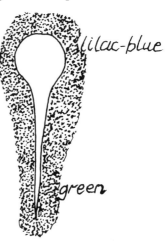

coming down to the end of the spine, we have a more distinctly greenish shade.

This I wish to state as a fact, along with what has been said to-day in connection with a purely external observation of the human form and of human conduct. Following this, we shall endeavour to observe also that other part of the human being which is attached to the portion we have discussed to-day, in the form of neck, trunk, limbs, etc., as constituting the second part of the human duality, to the end that we may then be able to proceed to a consideration of what is presented to us in the complete interaction of this human duality.

HUMAN DUALITY

21st March, 1911.

We shall encounter again and again, in the course of our reflections, the difficulty of keeping in our mind's eye ever
more exactly the exterior organism of man, in order that we
may learn to know the transitory, the perishable. But we
shall also see that this very road will lead us to a knowledge
of the imperishable, the eternal in human nature. Also it will
be necessary, in order to attain this goal, to sustain the effort
of looking upon the exterior human organism in all reverence,
as a revelation of the spiritual world.

When once we have permeated ourselves in some measure
with spiritual-scientific concepts and feelings, we shall come
quite easily to the thought that the human organism in its
stupendous complexity must be the most significant expression, the greatest and most important manifestation, of
those forces which live and weave as Spirit throughout the
world. We shall, indeed, have to find our way upward ever
more and more from the outer to the inner.

We have already seen that external observations, both from
the point of view of the layman and from that of the scientific
inquirer, must lead us to look upon man in a certain sense as
a duality. We have characterised this duality of the human
being—only hastily yesterday, to be sure, for we shall have to
go into this still more accurately—as being enclosed within the
protecting bony sheath of the skull and the spinal vertebrae.
We have seen that, if we ascend beyond the exterior form of

this part of man, we may gain a preliminary view of the connection between the life which we call our waking life of day,
and that other life, in the first place very full of uncertainty
for us, which we call the life of dreams. And we have seen
that the external forms of that portion of human nature which
we have described give us a kind of image, signify in a way a
revelation, on the one hand of dream-life, the chaotic life of
pictures; and on the other hand the waking day life, which is
endowed with the capacity to observe in sharp outlines.

To-day we shall first cast a fleeting glance over that part of
the human duality which may be found outside the region we
had in mind yesterday. Even the most superficial glance over
this second portion of the human being can teach us that this
portion really presents a picture in a certain respect the
opposite of the other one. In the brain and the spinal cord we
have the bony formation as the outer circumference, the
covering. If we consider the other portion of man's nature,
we are surely obliged to say that here we have the bony
formation disposed rather more within the organs. And yet
this would be only a very superficial observation. We shall be
carried deeper into the construction of this other portion of
man's nature if, for the moment, we keep the most important
systems of organs apart one from another, and compare
them, first, outwardly, with what we learned yesterday.

The systems of organs, or systems of instruments, of the
human organism to be considered first in this connection,
must be the apparatus of nutrition and all that lies between
this apparatus and that wonderful structure the heart, which
we readily experience as a sort of central point of the whole
human organism. And here even a superficial glance shows us
at once that these systems of instruments, especially the
apparatus of nutrition as we may call it in everyday speech,
are intended to take in the substances of our external, earthly

world and prepare them for further digestive work in the physical organism of man. We know that this apparatus of digestion begins by extending downward from the mouth, in the form of a tube, to the organ which everyone knows as the stomach. And a superficial observation teaches us that, from those articles of food which are conveyed through this canal into the stomach, the portions which are to a certain extent unassimilated are simply excreted, whereas other portions are carried over by the remaining digestive organs into the organism of the human body.

It is also well known that adjoining the actual digestive apparatus in the narrower sense of the term, and for the purpose of taking over from it in a transformed condition the nutritive substances with which it has been supplied, is what we may call the *lymph-system*. I shall at this point speak merely in outline. We may repeat accordingly that, adjoining the apparatus of nutrition in so far as this is attached chiefly to the stomach, there is this system of organs called the lymph-system, consisting of a number of canals, which in their turn spread over the whole body; and that this system takes over, in a certain way, what has been worked over by the rest of the digestive apparatus, and delivers it into the blood.

And then we have the third of these systems of organs, the blood-vessel system itself, with its larger and smaller tubes extending throughout the entire human organism and having the heart as the central point of all its work. We know also that, going out from the heart, those blood-vessels or blood-filled vessels which are called *arteries,* convey the blood to all parts of our organism; that the blood goes through a certain process in the separate parts of the human organism, and is carried back to the heart by means of other similar vessels which bring it back, however, in a transformed condition as so called "blue blood" in contrast to its red state. We know that this transformed blood, no longer useful for our life, is conducted from the heart into the lungs; that it there comes into contact with the oxygen taken up from the outer air; and that, by means of this, it is renewed in the lungs and conducted back again to the heart, to go its way afresh throughout the whole human organism.

If we are to consider these systems in their completeness, in order to have in our external method of observation a foundation for the occult method, let us begin by holding to that system which must, at the very outset, obviously be for everyone the central system of the entire human organism, namely, the blood-and-heart system. Let us, moreover, keep in mind that after the stale blood has been freshened in the lungs, transformed from blue blood into red blood, it returns once more to the heart and then goes out again from the heart as red blood, to be used in the organism. Notice, that everything which I intend to draw will be in mere outline, so that we shall be dealing only with diagrams.

Let us now briefly recall that the human heart is an organ which, properly speaking, consists in the first place of four parts or chambers, so separated by interior walls that one can distinguish between the two larger spaces lying below and the two smaller ones lying above, the two lower ones being the ventricles, as they are generally called, and the two upper ones the atria. I shall not speak about the "valves" to-day, but shall rather call attention, quite sketchily, to the course of the most important activities of the organ. And here, to begin with, one thing is clear: after the blood has streamed out of the left atrium into the left ventricle, it flows off through a large artery and from this point is conducted through the entire remainder of the organism. Now, let us bear in mind that this blood is first distributed to every separate organ of the whole organism; that it is then used up in this organism so that it is changed into the so-called blue blood, and as such returns to the right atrium of the heart; and that from there it flows into the right ventricle in order that it may go out again from this into the lungs, there again to be renewed and take a fresh course throughout the organism.

When we begin to visualise all this it is important, as a basis for an occult method of study, that we also add the fact that what we may call a subsidiary stream branches out from the aorta very near the heart; that this subsidiary stream leads to the brain, thus providing for the upper organs, and from there leads back again in the form of stale blood into the right atrium; and that it is there transformed, as blood which has passed through the brain, so to speak, in the same way as that blood is transformed which comes from the remaining parts of the organism. Thus we have a smaller, subsidiary circulation of the blood, in which the brain is inserted, separate from the other main circulation which provides for the entire remaining organism. Now, it is of extraordinary importance for us to bear this fact in mind. For we can only arrive at an important conception, affording us a basis for everything that will enable us to ascend to occult heights, if at this point we first ask ourselves the following question: In the same way in which the upper organs are inserted in the smaller circulation, is there something similar inserted within the circulation of the blood which provides for the rest of the organism?

Here we come, as a matter of fact, to a conclusion which even the external, superficial method of study can supply, that is, that there is inserted in the large circulation of the blood the organ we call the spleen; that further on the liver is inserted; and, still further on, the organ which contains the gall prepared by the liver.

Now, when we ask about the functions of these organs,

external science answers by saying that the liver prepares the gall; that the gall flows out into the digestive canal, and takes part in digesting the food in such a way that this may then be taken up by the lymph-system and conducted over into the blood. Much less, however, does external science tell us with regard to the spleen, the third of the organs here considered as inserted in the main circulation. When we consider these organs, we must first pay attention to the fact that they have to

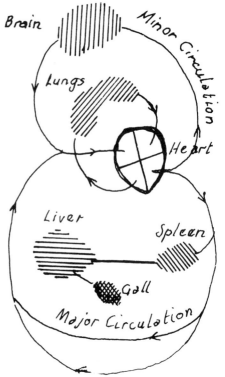

undertake the preparation of the nutritive matter for the human organism; but that, on the other hand, they are all three inserted as organs into the circulatory path of the blood. Their position within the circulation is not due to chance as nutritive matter is taken up into the blood, to be conveyed by means of the blood to the human organism in order to continuously supply this with substances to replace its metabolic material. These three organs participate in the whole metabolism of these nutritive substances.

Now arises the question: Can we already draw some sort of conclusion, from an external aspect, as to just how these organs take part in the joint activity of the human organism? Let us first fix our attention on this one external fact, namely, that these organs are inserted into the lower circulatory course of the blood in the same way in which the brain is inserted into the upper course; and let us now see for a moment, while first actually holding to this external method of study, which must later be deepened, whether it is possible that these organs really have a task similar to that of the brain. At the same time, wherein may such a task consist?

Let us begin by considering the upper portions of the human organism. It is these that receive the sense-impressions through the organs of sense, and work over the material contained in our sense-perceptions. We may say, therefore, that what takes place in the human head, in the upper part of the organism, is a working over of those impressions which flow in from outside through the sense-organs; and that what we may describe as the cause of everything that takes place in these upper parts is to be found in its essence in the external impressions or imprints. And, since these external impressions send their influences, together with what results from these influences in the working over of the outer impressions, into the upper organs of the organism, they therefore change the blood, or contribute to its change, and in their own way send this blood back to the heart transformed, just as the blood is sent back to the heart transformed from the rest of the organism.

Is it not obvious that we should now ask ourselves this other question: Since this upper part of the human organism opens outward by means of the sense-organs, opens doors to the outside world in the form of sense-organs, is there not a certain sort of correspondence between the working-in of the external world through these sense-organs upon the upper part of the human organism and that which works out of the three interior organs, the spleen, the liver, and the gall-bladder? Whereas, accordingly, the upper part of the organism opens outward in order to receive the influences of the outside world; and whereas the blood flows upwards, so to speak, in order to capture these impressions of the outside world, it flows downwards in order to take up what comes from these three organs. Thus we may say that, when we look out upon the world round about us, this world exercises its influence through our senses upon our upper organisation. And what thus flows in from outside, through the world of sense, we may think of as pressed together, contracted, as if into one centre; so that what flows into our organism from all sides is seen to be the same thing as that which flows out from the liver, the gall-bladder, and the spleen, namely, transformed outside world. If you go further into this matter you will see that it is not such a very strange reflection.

Imagine to yourselves the different sense-impressions that stream into us; imagine these contracted, thickened or condensed, formed into organs and placed inside us. Thus the blood presents itself inwardly to the liver, gall-bladder and spleen, in the same way as the upper part of the human organism presents itself to the outside world. And so we have the outside world which surrounds our sense-organs above, condensed as it were into organs that are placed in the interior of man, so that we may say: At one moment the world is working from outside, streaming into us, coming into contact with our blood in the upper organs, acting upon our blood; and the next moment that which is in the macrocosm works mysteriously in those organs into which it has first contracted itself, and there, from the opposite direction, acts upon our blood, presenting itself again in the same way as it does in the upper organs.

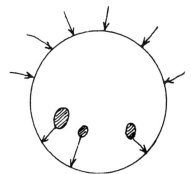

If we were to draw a sketch of this, we could do it by imagining the world on the one hand, acting from all directions upon our senses, and the blood exposing itself like a tablet to the impressions of this world; that would be our upper organism. And now let us imagine that we could contract this whole outer world into single organs, thus forming an extract of this world; that we could then transfer this extract into our interior in such a way that what is working from all directions now acts upon the blood from the other side of the tablet. We should then have formed in a most extraordinary way a pictorial scheme of the exterior and interior of the human organism. And we might already to a certain extent be able to say that the brain actually corresponds to our inner organism, in so far as this latter occupies the breast and the abdominal cavity. The world has, as it were, been placed in our inner man.

Even in this organisation, which we distinguish as a subordinate one, and which serves primarily for the carrying forward of the process of nutrition, we have something so mysterious as the fusion of the whole outer cosmos into a number of inner organs, inner instruments. And, if we now observe these organs more closely for a moment, the liver, the gall-bladder, and the spleen, we shall be able to say that the spleen is the first of these to offer itself to the bloodstream. This spleen is a strange organisation, embedded in plethoric tissue, and in this tissue there is a great number of tiny little granules —something which, in contrast to the rest of the mass of tissue, has the appearance of little white granules.

When we observe the relation between the blood and the spleen, the latter appears to us like a sieve through which the blood passes in order that it may offer itself to an organ of the kind which, in a certain sense, is a shrivelled-up portion of the macrocosm. Again, the spleen stands in connection with the liver. At the next stage we see how the blood offers itself to the liver, and how the liver in its turn, as a third step, secretes the gall, which then goes over into the nutritive substances, and from there comes with the transformed nutritive substances into the blood.

This offering of itself on the part of the blood to these organs we cannot think of in any but the following way: The organ which first meets the blood is the spleen, the second is the liver, and the third is the gall-bladder, which has really a very complicated relation to the entire blood system, in that the gall is given over to the food and takes part in its digestion. On such grounds, the occultists of all times have given certain names to these organs. Now, I beg of you most earnestly not to think of anything special for the time being in connection with these names, but rather to think of them only as names that were originally given to these organs and to disregard the fact that the names signify also something else in connection with these organs. Later on we shall see why just these names were chosen. Because the spleen is the first of the three organs to present itself to the blood—we can say this by way of a purely external comparison—it appeared to the occultists of old to be best designated by the name belonging to that star which, to these ancient occultists and their observations, was the first within our solar system to show itself in cosmic space. For this reason they called the spleen "saturnine," or an *inner Saturn* in man; and, similarly, the liver they called an *inner Jupiter*; and the gall-bladder, an *inner Mars*. Let us begin by thinking of nothing in connection with these names, except that we have chosen them because we have arrived at the concept, at first hypothetical, that the external worlds, which otherwise are accessible rather to our senses, have been contracted into these organs and that in these organs *inner* worlds, so to speak, come to meet us, just as outer worlds meet us in the planets. We may now be able to say that, just as the external worlds show themselves as acting upon the blood-system in that they influence that for which the blood-system is there.

We shall find, to be sure, a significant difference between what we spoke of yesterday as the peculiarities of the human brain and that which here appears to us as a sort of inner cosmic system. This difference lies simply in the fact that man, to begin with, knows nothing about what takes place within his lower organism: that is, he knows nothing about the impressions which the inner worlds, or planets, as we may call them, make upon him, whereas the very characteristic of the other experience is that the outer worlds do make their impressions upon his consciousness. In a certain respect, therefore, we may call these inner worlds the realm of the unconscious, in contrast to the conscious realm we have learned to know in the life of the brain.

Now, precisely that which lies in this "conscious" and this "unconscious" is more clearly explained when we employ something else to assist us. We all know that external science states that the organ of consciousness is the nerve-system, together with all that pertains to it. Now we must bear in mind, as a basis for our occult study, a certain relationship which the nerve-system has to the blood-system, that is, to what we have to-day considered in a sketchy way. We then see that our nerve-system everywhere enters in ways into relation with our blood-system, that the blood everywhere presses upon our nerve-system. Moreover, we must here first take notice of something which external science in this connection holds to be already established. This science looks upon it as a settled matter that in the nerve-system is to be found the sole and entire regulator of all activity of consciousness, of everything, that is, which we characterise as "soul-life." We cannot here refrain from recalling, although at first only by way of allusion for the purpose of authenticating this later on, that for the occultist the nerve-system exists only as a sort of basis for consciousness. For precisely in the same way that the nerve-system is a part of our organism and comes into contact with the blood-system, or at least bears a certain relation to it, so do the ego and that which we call the astral body make themselves a part of the whole human being. And even an external ob-servation, which has frequently been employed in my lectures, can show us that the nerve-system is in a certain way a manifestation of the astral body. Through such an observation we can see that, in the case of ordinary inanimate beings in nature, we can ascribe only a physical body to that part of their being which they present to us. When, however, we ascend from inanimate, inorganic natural bodies to animate natural bodies, to organisms, we are obliged to suppose that these organisms are permeated by the so-called ether-body, or life-body, which contains in itself the causes of the phenomena of life. We shall see later on that anthroposophy, or occultism, does not speak of the ether-body, or life-body, in the same way that people in the past spoke of "life-force." Rather does anthroposophy, when it speaks of the ether-body, speak of something which the spiritual eye actually sees, that is, of something real underlying the external physical body. When we consider the plants we are obliged to attribute to them an ether-body. And, if we ascend from the plants to sentient beings, to the animals, we find that it is this element of sentiency, of inner life, or, better still, of inner experience, which primarily differentiates the animal externally from the plant. If mere life-activity, which cannot yet sense itself inwardly, cannot yet attain to the kindling of sentienie, to sense life inwardly, the astral body must become a part of the animal's organism. And in the nerve-system, which the plants do not yet have, we must recognise the external instrument of the astral body, which in turn is the spiritual prototype of the nerve-system. As the archetype is related to its manifestation, to its image, so is the astral body related to the nerve-system.

Now when we come to man—and I said yesterday that in occultism our task is not as simple as it is for the external scientific method in which everything can, so to speak, be jumbled together—we must always, when we study the human organs, be aware of the fact that these organs, or systems of organs, are capable of being put to certain uses for which the corresponding systems of organs in the animal organism, even when these appear similar, cannot be used. At this point we shall merely affirm in advance what will appear later as having a still more profound basis, that, in the case of man, we must designate the blood as an external instrument for the ego, for all that we denote as our inner-most soul-centre, the ego; so that in the nerve-system we have an external instrument of the astral body, and in our blood an external instrument of the ego. Just as the nerve-system in our organism enters into certain relations with the blood, so do those inner soul faculties which we experience in ourselves as our representations, feelings or sensations, etc., enter into a certain relation with our ego.

The nerve-system is differentiated in the human organism in manifold ways; the inner nerve-fibres at the points where these develop into nerves of hearing, of seeing, for example show us how great its differentiation is. The nervous-system is something that extends throughout the organism in such a way as to comprehend the most manifold inner diversities. A study of the blood as it streams through the organism shows us, that, even taking into account the transformation from red into blue blood, it is, nevertheless, a uniform entity in the whole organism. With this characteristic unity, it comes into contact with the differentiated nerve-system, just as does the ego with the differentiated soul-life, for it also is made up of representations, sensations, will-impulses, feelings and the like. The further you pursue this comparison—and it is given meanwhile only as a comparison— the more clearly you will be shown ·that a far-reaching similarity exists in the relations of the two archetypes, the ego and the astral body, to their respective images, the blood-system and the nerve-system. Now, of course, one may say at this point that blood is certainly blood everywhere. However, it undergoes certain changes in flowing through the organism; it is possible to draw a parallel between these changes that take place in the blood and what goes on in the ego. But our ego is an entity. As far back as we can remember in our life between birth and death we can say: "This ego was always present, in our fifth year just as in our sixth year, yesterday just as to-day. It is the same ego." And yet, if we now look into what this ego contains, we shall discover this fact: This ego that lives in me is filled with a sum-total of representations, sensations, feelings, etc., which are to be attributed to the astral body and which come into contact with the ego. A year ago this ego was filled with a different content, yesterday it contained still another, and to-day its content is again different. Thus the ego, we see, comes into contact with the entire soul-content, streams through this entire soul-content. And, just as the

blood streams through the whole organism and comes everywhere into contact with the differentiated nerve-system, so
does the ego meet with the differentiated life of the soul,
in representations, feelings, will-impulses and the like. Already,
therefore, this simple comparative method of study shows us
that there is some justification in looking upon the blood
system as an image of the ego, and the nerve system as an
image of the astral body, as higher, supersensible members
of the nature of man, while the etheric body connects itself
more with the physical body.

It is necessary for us to remember that the blood streams
throughout the organism in the manner already indicated;
that on the one side it presents itself to the outer world
like a tablet facing the impressions of the outer world; on
the other side, it faces what we have called the inner world.
And indeed it is so also with our ego. We first direct this ego
of ours toward the outside world and receive impressions
from it. There results from this a great variety of content
within the ego; it is filled with these impressions coming from
outside. There are also such moments when the ego retires
within itself and is given up to its pain and suffering, pleasure
and happiness, inner feelings and so forth, when it permits
what it is not receiving at this moment directly through
contact with the external world, but what it carries within
itself, to arise in the memory. So, in this connection also,
we find a parallel between the blood and the ego; for the
blood, like a tablet, presents itself at one time to the outside
world and at another time to the inner world; and we could
accordingly represent this ego by a simple sketch* exactly
as we have represented the blood. We can bring the external
impressions which the ego receives, when we think of them
as concepts, as soul-pictures in general, into the same sort
*See page 35.

of relation to the ego as that which we have brought about between our blood and the real external occurrences coming to us through the senses. That is we could bring what is related to the soul-life into connection with the ego, exactly as we have done in the case of the physical bodily life and the blood.

Let us now study the co-operation, the mutual interaction, between the blood and the nerves, from this standpoint. If we consider the eye, we see that outer impressions act upon this organ. The impressions of colour and light act upon the optic nerve. So long as they affect the optic nerve, having for themselves an active instrument in the nerve-system, we are able to affirm that they have an effect upon the astral body. We may state that, at the moment when a relationship occurs between the nerves and the blood, the parallel process which takes place in the soul is that the manifold representations within the life of the soul come into connection with the ego. When, therefore, we consider this relationship between the nerves and the blood, we may represent by another diagram how that which streams in from outside through the nerves when we see an object, forms a certain connection with that part of the circulation of the blood which come into the region of the optic nerve.

This relationship is something of extraordinary importance for us, if we wish to observe the human organism in such a way that our observation shall provide a basis for arriving at the occult foundations of the human being. In ordinary life the process that takes place is such that

each influence transmitted by means of the nerves inscribes itself in the blood, as on a tablet, and in doing so records itself in the instrument of the ego. Let us suppose for a moment, however, that we should artificially put a man in such a condition that the activity of the nerve should be severed from the circulation of the blood, so that they could no longer act upon each other. We can indicate this by a diagram in which the two parts are shown more widely separated, so that a reciprocal action between the nerves and the blood can no longer take place. In this case the condition may be such that no impression can be made upon the nerve. Something of this sort can be brought about if, for example, the nerve is cut. If, indeed, it should come to pass by some means that no impression is made upon the nerve, then it is also not strange if the man himself is unable to experience anything espe-cial through this nerve. But let us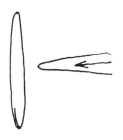
suppose that in spite of the interrup-ting of the connection between the nerve and the blood a certain impression
is made upon the nerve. This can be brought to pass through an external experiment by stimulating the nerve by means of an electric current. Such an external influence on the nerve does not, however, concern us here. But there is still another way of affecting the nerve under conditions in which it cannot act upon the course of the blood normally connected with it.

It is possible to bring about such a condition of the human organism; and this is done in a particular way, by means of certain representations, emotions and feelings which the human being has experienced and made a part of himself, and which, if this inner experiment is to be truly successful,

ought, properly speaking, to be really lofty, moral or intel-
lectual ideas. When a man practises a rigorous inner concentration of the soul on such imaginative representatives,
and if he does this in a state of waking consciousness, forming
these into symbols let us say, it then happens that he takes
complete control of the nerve and, as a result of this inner
concentration, draws it back to a certain extent from the
course of the blood. For when man simply gives himself up
to normal, external impressions, the natural connection
between the nerve and the circulation is present; but if, in
strict concentration upon his ego, he holds fast to what he
obtains in a normal way, apart from all external impressions and apart from what the outside world brings about
in the ego, he then has something in his soul which can
have originated only in the consciousness and is the content
of consciousness, and which makes a special demand upon
the nerve and separates its activity then and there from its
connection with the activity of the blood. The consequence
of this is that, by means of such inner concentration, which
actually breaks the connection between the nerve and the
blood, that is, when it is so strong that the nerve is in a
certain sense freed from its connection with the blood-
system, the nerve is at the same time freed from that for
which the blood is the external instrument, namely, from
the ordinary experiences of the ego. And it is indeed a fact—
this finds its complete experimental support through the
inner experiences of that spiritual training designed to lead
upward into the higher worlds—that as a result of such
concentration the entire nerve-system is separated from the
blood-system and from its ordinary tasks in connection with
the ego. It then happens, as the particular consequence of
this, that whereas the nerve-system had previously written
its action upon the tablet of the blood, it now permits what

it contains within itself as a working force to return into itself, and does not permit it to reach the blood. It is, therefore, possible purely through processes of inner concentration, to separate the blood-system from the nerve-system, and thereby to cause that which, pictorially expressed, would otherwise have flowed into the ego, to course back again into the nerve-system.

Now, the peculiar thing is that when the human being once actually brings this about through such inward exertion of the soul, he has then an entirely different sort of inner experience. He stands before a completely changed horizon of consciousness which we may attempt to describe as follows: When the nerve and the blood have an appropriate connection with each other, as is the case in normal life, man brings into relation with the ego the impressions which come from within his inner being and those which come from the outer world. The ego then conserves those forces which reach out along the entire horizon of consciousness, and everything is related to the ego. But when, through inner concentration, he separates his nerve-system, lifts it, that is to say, through inner soul-forces out of his blood-system, he does not then live in his ordinary ego. He cannot then say "I" with respect to that which he calls his "Self," in the same sense in which he had previously said "I" in his ordinary normal consciousness. It then seems to the man as if he had quite consciously lifted a portion of his real being out of himself, as if something which he does not ordinarily see, which is supersensible and works in upon his nerves, does not now impress itself upon his blood-tablet or make impression upon his ordinary ego. He feels himself lifted away from the entire blood-system, raised up, as it were, out of his organism; and he meets something different as a substitute for what he has experienced in the blood-system.

Whereas the nerve-activity was previously impressed upon in the blood-system, it is now reflected back into itself. He is now living in something different; he feels himself in another ego, another Self, which before this could at best be merely divined. He feels a supersensible world uplifted within him.

If once more we draw a sketch, showing the relation between the blood and the nerve, or the entire nerve-system, as this receives into itself the impressions from the outside world, this may be done in the following way.

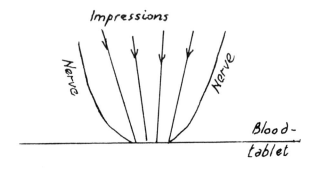

The normal impressions would then impress themselves in the blood-system, and thus be within it. If, however, we have removed the nerve-system, nothing goes into the blood-system; everything flows back again into the nerve-system; and thus a world has opened to us of which we had previously no intimation. It has opened as far as the terminations of our nerve-system, and we feel the recoil. To be sure, only he can feel this recoil who goes through the necessary soul-exercises. In the case of the normal consciousness, man feels that he takes into himself whatever sort of world happens to face him, so that everything is inscribed upon the blood-system as on a tablet, and he then lives in his ego with these impressions. In the other case, however, he goes with these impressions only to that point where the terminations of the nerves offer him an inner resistance. Here, at the nerve-terminals, he rebounds as it were, and experiences himself in the outside world. Thus, when we have a colour impression, which we receive through the eye, it passes into the optic nerve, impresses itself upon the tablet of the blood, and we feel what we express as a fact when we say: "I see red." But now, after we have made ourselves capable of doing so,

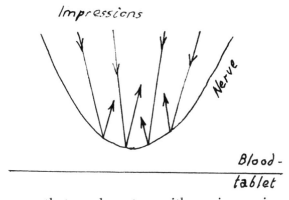

Impressions

Nerve

Blood-tablet

let us suppose that we do not go with our impressions as far as the blood, but only to the terminations of the nerves; that at this point we rebound into our inner life, rebound before we reach the blood. In that case we live, as a matter of fact, only as far as our eye, our optic nerve. We recoil before the bodily expression of our blood, we live outside Self and are actually within the light-rays which penetrate our eyes. Thus we have actually come out of ourselves; indeed, we have accomplished this by reason of the fact that we do not penetrate as deep down into our Self as we ordinarily do, but rather go only as far as the nerve-terminals. The effect on a soul-life such as this, if we have brought it to the stage where we turn back at the terminations of the nerves into our inner being, so that we do not go as far as our blood; whereas otherwise the normal consciousness of the inner man ordinarily goes down into the blood, and the soul-life identifies itself with the physical man, feels itself at one with him.

As a result of these external observations we have to-day succeeded in disconnecting the entire blood-system, which we have thought of as a kind of tablet that presents itself on the one side to the external, on the other side to the internal impressions, from what we may call the higher man, the man we may become if we find release from our Selves and become free. Now, we shall best be able to study the whole inner nature of this blood-system if we do not make use of general phrases, but observe what exists as reality in man, namely the supersensible, invisible man to whom we can lift ourselves when we go only as far as the terminations of our nerves, and if we also observe man as he is when he goes all the way into the blood. For we can then advance further, to the thought that man can really live in the outside world, that he can pour himself out over the whole external world, can go forth into this world and view from the reverse standpoint, as it were, the inner man, or what is usually meant by that term. In short, we shall learn to know the functions of the blood, and of those organs which are inserted into the circulatory course of the blood, when we can answer the following questions: What does a more accurate knowledge show us, when that which comes from a higher world, to which man can raise himself, is portrayed upon the tablet of the blood? It shows us that everything connected with the life of the blood is the very central point of the human being, when, without coining phrases, but rather looking only at sensible as well as supersensible realities, we consider carefully the relationship of this wonderful system to a higher world. For this is in truth to be our task: to learn to see clearly the whole visible physical Man as an image of that other "Man" who is rooted and lives in the spiritual world. We shall thereby come to find that the human organism is one of the truest images of that Spirit which lives in the universe, and we shall attain to a very special understanding of that Spirit.

CO-OPERATION IN THE HUMAN DUALITY

22nd March, 1911.

These first three lectures, including to-day's, are intended to orientate us in a general way in regard to what must be considered in connection with the life of man, with his true being. This is why some of the more important concepts are, in a sense, left hanging in the air, having been merely stated, since then more detailed exposition will have to follow later. But it is better to make a general survey of the whole method of occult observation of the human being and then to build into our study, which for the present we accept only as hypothetical, that which will then become clear to us as its deeper foundations.

I have already dwelt upon one matter, at the close of yesterday's lecture. There I endeavoured to show that, by means of certain soul-exercises, by means of intensive concentration of thought and feeling, the human being can call forth a state of life different from the ordinary one. The ordinary state expresses itself as it does because in our fully waking day consciousness, we have a normal relationship between the nerves and the blood. That which happens by way of the nerves inscribes itself upon the tablet of the blood. By means of soul-exercises, a man may reach the point where he can so completely control the nerve that it does not extend its activity as far as the blood. This activity is thrown back into the nerve itself. But now, because the blood is the instrument of the ego, a person who does this, who has freed his nerve-system from the course of the blood through intensive concentration of feeling and thought, feels as if he were estranged from his own accustomed being, lifted out of it. He feels as if he now stood facing himself, with the result that he can no longer say to this familiar being of his, "This is I"; he must say, "That is you." Thus he stands facing his own Self just as he might face any unfamiliar person living in the physical world.

A man like this, who has become in a certain sense clairvoyant, feels as if a higher order of being were towering up in his soul-life. This is an entirely different feeling from that which a man has when he confronts the ordinary world. When he confronts the external world, he feels that he stands as a stranger facing the things and being of this external world, the animals, the plants, etc.—as a being who stands beside them or outside them. He knows quite definitely when he has a flower before him: "The flower is there, and I am here." It is otherwise when, as a result of the liberation from his nerve-system, he ascends into the spiritual world, when he lifts himself out of his ego. He does not any longer feel in that case: "There is the strange-being that faces me, and here am I," but rather as if the other being entered completely into him, and as if he felt himself one with it. Thus we may say that the clairvoyant human being learns, through advanced power of observation, to know the spiritual world—that spiritual world with which man is, indeed, connected and which to a certain extent, comes to meet him by way of the nerve-system, even though in normal life this occurs by the indirect road of the sense-impressions. It is the spiritual world, therefore, about which the human being in his ordinary consciousness at first knows nothing, and it is this same spiritual world which, nevertheless, actually inscribes itself upon the tablet of our blood, hence upon our ego. In other words, we may say that underlying everything that surrounds us externally in the world of sense there lies a spiritual world, so that we see as though through a veil woven by the sense-impressions. In our normal consciousness, which is compassed by the horizon of our ordinary ego, we do not see the spiritual world lying behind this veil. The moment, however, that we free ourselves of the ego, the ordinary sense-impressions disappear also. We then begin to live in a spiritual world above us, that same world that exists in reality behind the sense-impressions, and with which we become one when we lift our nerve-system out of our ordinary blood-system.

We have now followed in a manner the process of human life, how it is stimulated from the external world and how it carries on its work through the nerves and the blood. At the same time, we have called attention to the fact that we can see in the purely organic, physical inner life of man a kind of "compressed outside world"; and we have pointed in particular to the fact that such an outside world, condensed into organs, is present in our liver, our gall-bladder, and our spleen. We may say, therefore, that just as the blood in the one direction, in the upper extremity of our organism, course courses through the brain in order there to come into contact with the outside world (this takes place by reason of the fact that the external sense-impressions work upon the brain) just so, as it circulates through the body, does it come into relationship with the inner organs among which we have first considered the liver, the gall-bladder, and the spleen. The blood does not in these organs come into contact with any sort of outside world because they do not open outward as do the organs of sense, but are enclosed within the organism, are covered on all sides and consequently develop only an inner life. Moreover, these organs can act upon the blood only in accordance with their own nature as liver, gall-bladder, spleen. They do not, like the eye or the ear, receive outside impressions, and they cannot, therefore, pass on to the blood influences stimulated from outside, but can simply express their own particular natures through whatever effect these may have upon the blood. When we observe this inner world into which the outside world is condensed, as it were, we may state that here an outer world which has become an inner world acts upon the human blood where it can act at all.

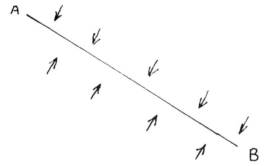

If we draw a sketch of this, and represent the tablet of the blood by the line A B, we have to represent everything which comes from outside as now directed in a certain sense inward, and pressing from the one direction against the tablet of the blood, while being, as it were, inscribed upon one side of the tablet, whereas everything coming from the inside we have to think of as approaching from the other direction and inscribing itself on the other side of the tablet. Or doing it less schematically, we might then take the human head and observe the blood as it courses through this in such a way that we say: "It is being written upon from outside through the sense-organs; and the brain, in performing its task, has the same sort of transforming influence upon the blood as the inner organs have." For these three organs, the liver, the gall-bladder and the spleen, work, as we know from the opposite direction, from the other side, upon the blood flowing into them. Thus it would seem that the blood may be able to receive radiations and influences from the inner organs, and by means, supposing this to be possible, it can, as the instrument of the ego, bring to expression in this ego the inner life of these organs, just as everything which surrounds us in the world outside finds expression in the life of our brain.

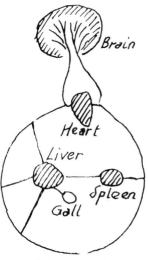

At this point we must understand clearly, that something else very definite must happen to make possible the action of these organs upon the blood. Let us remember that we had to assert that only through the reciprocal activity, through the connection between the nerve and the course of the blood, can there be any possibility whatever that anything will be inscribed upon the blood, that any influence can be exercised upon it. If therefore from the other direction, from the inner side, influences are to be exercised upon the blood, if the inner organs, or what we may call man's inner cosmic system, are to work upon the blood, there must be inserted between these organs and the blood something similar to a nerve-system. The "inner world" must first be able to act upon a nerve-system if it is to carry its activity over to the blood. Thus we see, by simply comparing the lower portion of the human being with the upper, that we are forced to presuppose that something in the nature of a nerve-system must be inserted between the circulating blood and our inner organs—among which we have here these three representative ones, the liver, the gall-bladder, and the spleen.

External observation shows us that this really is the case, that in all these organs is inserted what is called the "sympathetic nervous system" which extends throughout the bodily cavity of man, and which stands in a relationship to his inner world and to the course of the blood similar to that in which the nervous system of the spinal cord stands to the great outside world and to the life of man, to the circulation of his blood. This sympathetic nervous system passes first along the spine and, going out from there, traverses the most widely separated parts of the organism and branches out, spreading into reticular forms, especially in the abdominal cavity, where one part of it goes by the popular name of the "solar plexus." We may expect to find a certain variation of this system from the other nerve-system. It is always interesting, even if it should not serve as any proof, to ask ourselves: What would be the relation between this nerve-system and the nerve-system of the spinal cord if those conditions should be fulfilled which we have for the present asserted hypothetically? It would be obvious that, just as the nerve-system of the spinal cord must open itself to surrounding space, so would this sympathetic nerve-system have to incline toward what is compressed into the inner organisation. Thus the nerve-system of the spinal cord is related to the sympathetic nerve-system, that is, if the

facts agree with our presuppositions, somewhat as lines radiating outward in all directions from the circumference of a circle (a) would be related to those radii that we might direct away from the centre of the circle toward its circum-

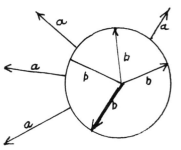

ference (*b*). In a certain sense, therefore, there would have to
be an antithesis between the sympathetic nerve-system and
the nerve-system of the brain and spinal cord. This antithesis actually does exist. We see here that it may be of
great value to us to be able to point to the fact that, if our
assumptions are correct, experience and observation will in a
manner confirm them. And, when we turn our attention
again to what we have been observing, it is evident that external observation does confirm the suppositions we have
formed. We find that, whereas in the case of the sympathetic
nerve-system the essential thing is that ganglia of a certain
kind form themselves which are strong and large, while the
connecting filaments radiating out from these are relatively
small and of little account in contrast to these ganglia,
exactly the reverse is true in the case of the nerve-system of
the brain and spinal cord. There the connecting threads are
the important thing, whereas the ganglia have a subordinate
significance.

Thus our observation does, in fact, confirm what we
accepted as a supposition, and we can now make the following
assertion. If the function of the sympathetic nerve-system
must consist in carrying over to the blood the inner life of
the human organism, which expresses itself in the nourishing
and the warming through of the organism, and which pours
itself into the sympathetic nerves, in exactly the same way
in which the outer impressions are carried over to the tablet
of the blood by means of the nerve-system of the brain and
spinal cord, in that case we obtain through the instrument of
the ego, which is the blood, by the roundabout way of the
sympathetic nerve-system, the impressions of our own inner
body. Since however this inner body of ours, like everything
physical, is built up out of the spirit, we therefore take up
into our ego, by the roundabout road of the sympathetic

nerve-system, what has been condensed as spiritual world into the corresponding organs of the inner world of man.

Thus we see here also, strangely enough, how that duality in the human being with which we began our studies is expressed in even greater exactness. We see the world at one moment outside; at another moment we see it inside. Both times we see this world working in such a way that it uses a nerve-system as the instrument of its work. We see that in the centre, between the outside world and the inside world, is placed our blood-system which exposes its two sides, to be written upon like a tablet, sometimes from outside, sometimes from inside.

We said yesterday and repeat to-day for the sake of clarity, that the human being is in position to free his nerves, in so far as these lead to the outside world, from their action upon the blood-system. We must now put the question, whether something similar is possible also in the other direction. And we shall see later that it is possible, as a matter of fact, to practise also other exercises of the soul that are capable of producing in the other direction the same effect as that of which we have spoken. There is one difference, however, in connection with the effect produced in this other direction. Whereas we are able through concentration of thought, concentration of feeling, and occult exercises, to set free from the blood the nerves of our brain and spinal cord, we are able, on the other hand, by means of such concentrations as go right down into our inner life, our inner world—by which is meant in particular that sort of concentration included under the term "the mystical life,"—to penetrate so deep down within ourselves that in doing so we most certainly do not ignore our ego, nor therefore its instrument the blood. The mystical immersion, concerning which we know that by its means a man plunges down, so to speak, into his own divine being, into his own spirituality in so far as this is alive in him, this mystical immersion is not primarily a lifting of oneself out of the ego. It is rather a positive plunging of oneself down into the ego, a strengthening or energising of the ego-feeling. We can convince ourselves of this if we set aside what the mystics of the present day may say, and consider to some extent the earlier mystics.

These earlier mystics, whether they had for their foundation more of reality or less matters not, endeavoured, above all things, to penetrate into their own ego and to look away from everything which the outside world could offer, in order to be free from all external impressions and to plunge down completely into themselves. This inward self-communion, this diving down into one's own organism. This now works further upon the entire organisation of the human being; and we may say that this inward immersion, which may be called in the true sense of the term the "mystic path," is in direct contrast to that other path leading out into the macrocosm, so that we do not draw the instrument of the ego, which is the blood, away from the nerve, but on the contrary thrust it more than ever against the sympathetic nerve-system. Whereas, therefore, we loosen by means of the process described yesterday the connection between the nerve and the blood, we here strengthen the connection between the blood and the sympathetic nerve-system by means of true mystic immersion.

This is the physiological counterpart: that the blood is here pressed in more than ever against the sympathetic nerve-system; whereas, when the wish is to reach the spiritual world in the other way, the blood is pushed away from the nerve. Thus we see that what can take place in the mystic immersion is primarily an impressing of the blood upon this inner, sympathetic nerve-system.

Now, let us suppose that we might disregard what happens when a man thus enters into his inner being, when he does not free himself from his ego, but presses down, on the contrary, into the ego, and takes with him at the same time all his less desirable qualities. For when a man frees himself from his ego he leaves the ego behind with all these less desirable qualities; but when he immerses himself into his ego it is not at all certain, to begin with, that he does not at the same time press down all his undesirable characteristics into this energised ego of his: in other words, that everything contained in his passionate blood is not pressed down with the blood into the sympathetic nerve-system. But let us suppose that we might for the time being disregard all this, and assume that the mystic has taken care, before coming to any such mystic immersion, that his less desirable qualities shall have disappeared more and more and that, in place of these egoistic qualities, selfless, altruistic feelings have appeared; that he has prepared himself by endeavouring to bring to life within himself a feeling of compassion for all things possessed of being to the end that, by means of the selfless qualities that have thus been called forth for all beings, he may paralyse these other qualities that take account only of the ego. Let us suppose, then, that the man has prepared himself sufficiently for this immersion within his own inner being. He carries his ego in that case by means of the instrument of his blood down into his own inner world. It then comes to pass that his inner nerve-system, the sympathetic nerve-system, about which the human being in his normal consciousness knows nothing, presses its way into the ego-consciousness, so that he begins to know: "I have within me something which can mediate to me the inner world in a similar way to that in which the other nerve-system mediates the outer world to me."

Thus man descends into his own being and becomes aware, so to speak, of his sympathetic nerve-system. And just as he can know, by means of the outer nerve-system of the brain and spinal cord, the outside world that forms his environment, so there now comes to meet him that inner world which has built itself up within him. Moreover, just as we do not see the nerves, since no one sees the optic nerve, but rather that which is to be seen by means of the nerve, the external world that penetrates into our consciousness, just so also in the case of the mystic immersion it is not, to begin with, the inner nerves that penetrate the consciousness, for the human being is aware only that he has in these an instrument through which he can behold what is within him. It is indeed, something quite different that appears. Now that he has brought his faculty of cognition to an inward clairvoyance, his inner world appears before him. Just as the outward-directed look discloses to us the outer world, and our nerves do not in the process come into our consciousness, so likewise it is not our sympathetic nerve-system that comes into our consciousness, but obviously that which confronts us as "inner world." Only this inner world, which here comes into our consciousness is really *our own Self as physical man.*

Perhaps it is not so much to the point here, but I should feel inclined to suggest that a thinker who is the least materialistic might, indeed, sense a feeling of horror rising up within him if he were to say to himself: "In that case I can see my own organism from within!" And what he might mean, perhaps, would be: "How wonderful, to become clairvoyant by means of my sympathetic nerve-system and to be able to see my own liver, gall-bladder, and spleen!" As I remarked, this is not necessarily to the point, yet some-one might say such a thing. But the facts are otherwise. For, in making an objection like this, such a person would fail to

take into account that what the human being ordinarily calls
in external life his liver, his gall-bladder, and his spleen is
viewed from *outside,* just like all other external objects. In
ordinary life we are obliged to view the human organism
through the external senses, the outer nerves. What we may
learn to know in anatomy, in the usual physiology, as liver,
gall-bladder, and spleen constitutes these organs as seen from
outside by means of the nerve-system of the brain and spinal
cord. There they are viewed in exactly the same way in which
one views anything externally. The position is entirely
different, however, when a man can see clairvoyantly *inside*
himself by means of the sympathetic nerve-system. He does
not in that case see at all the same things that one sees when
looking from outside; rather, he now sees something which
caused the seers throughout the ages to choose such strange
names as those I cited in the second lecture.

He is now aware that in reality, to external sight which
uses the brain and the spinal cord, these organs appear in
Maya, in external illusion, because the aspect they offer
outwardly does not show them in their inner essential significance. He sees, in fact, something entirely different when
he is able to observe this his inner world from the opposite
direction, but now with the use of an inwardly clairvoyant
eye. He now gradually realises why the seers of all times
connected the activity of the spleen with the action of
Saturn, the activity of the liver with the action of Jupiter,
and the activity of the gall-bladder with the action of Mars.
For what he thus sees in his own inner self is, indeed, fundamentally different from what presents itself to the external
view. He becomes aware that he actually has before him
portions of the outside world enclosed within the boundaries
of his inner organs.

And one thing now becomes particularly clear, which may

serve us chiefly as an example for this method of arriving at knowledge, enabling us to see what course these ways of attaining knowledge follow in the life of the organism, in leading us beyond the customary views. In this case we can convince ourselves especially with regard to one fact, namely, how very significant an organ the human spleen is. Indeed, this organ really appears to inner observation as if it did not consist of an externally visible substance, of fleshly matter, but rather, if the expression may be permitted, although it approximates only to what can actually be observed, as if it actually were a luminous cosmic body in miniature with every possible sort of inner life, and indeed an inner life highly complicated.

Yesterday I called your attention to the fact that the spleen, externally observed, may be described as a plethoric tissue with minute white corpuscles embedded in it, so that it is legitimate, perhaps, from the point of view of external observation, to assume that the blood which flows through the spleen is strained through it as if through a sieve. When this spleen is observed *inwardly*, on the other hand, it appears above all to be an organ which, by means of the manifold inner forces already mentioned, is brought into a continual rhythmic movement. We convince ourselves even in connection with such an organ as this that a very great deal in the world is, as a matter of fact, dependent upon *rhythm*. An intimation of the importance of rhythm in the entire life of the world may be felt when we recognise it also externally in the pulse-beat of the blood. In that case, however, it is externally that we recognise it. But we can follow it externally also in the spleen. For it is possible here to follow it rather exactly, and we can also look for confirmation of what has been said through external observation. To inward clairvoyant sight all the differentiations of the spleen, which take place as if in a luminous body, are there in order to give this spleen a certain rhythm in life. This rhythm differs very considerably from other rhythms that we perceive elsewhere in life. Indeed it is just here, in the case of the spleen, that it is interesting to observe how very noticeably this rhythm differs from others: that is, it is far less regular than the other rhythms of which we shall speak later. This is due to the fact that the spleen lies near the human nutritive apparatus, and has something to do with this.

Now, you will be able to understand me if you consider how amazingly regular the rhythm of the blood must be in the human being in order that life may be properly sustained. This must be a very regular rhythm. But there is another rhythm that is regular only to a very slight degree—although one could wish that, through self-education of the human being, it might become more and more regular especially in the life of the child—namely, the rhythm of eating and drinking. Any man of moderately regular habits does, to be sure, keep a certain rhythm in this respect. He takes his breakfast, his midday meal, and his evening meal at certain times, and by doing so he follows, of course, a certain rhythm. But we know, alas, how it is with this rhythm in many another respect, through the humouring of the fastidiousness of many children who are simply given a thing whenever they crave it, regardless of all rhythm. Moreover, the fact that adults also are not very particular in observing a regular rhythm in connection with eating and drinking— there is not the slightest intention here of giving pedantic instruction in this matter, for our modern life does not always allow of rhythm—the fact that we fill ourselves with external nourishment with such irregularity, and that in our drinking especially we are so irregular, is sufficiently well known and need not be criticised but only mentioned. Yet,

AN OCCULT PHYSIOLOGY

on the other hand, that which we supply to our organism with such imperfect rhythm must gradually be changed in rhythm so that it will adapt itself to the more regular rhythm of this organism, it must be adapted, as it were. The grossest irregularity must be removed, and something like the following must come about. Let us suppose that, in order to regulate his daily schedule, a man is compelled to breakfast at eight o'clock and assume that this has become a habit. Now, suppose that he should go to see a friend, and that while there he should be invited, through a courtesy which cannot in general be too highly praised, to take something between these two meals. In this case he has interrupted his rhythm to a very decided extent, and thereby a certain definitive influence is exerted upon the rhythm of his external organism.

Now there must be something able to strengthen correspondingly whatever is regular in rhythm in the supplying of external nourishment and to weaken the influence of whatever is irregularly introduced. The worst irregularities must be counterbalanced. Accordingly somewhere along the course taken by the food as it goes over into the rhythm of the blood, there must be inserted an organ that equalises the irregularity of the process of nourishment in contrast with the necessary regularity of the rhythm of the blood. This organ is the spleen. Thus, by observing certain very definite rhythmic processes brought about by the spleen in this way we are able to get an idea of the fact that the spleen is really a "transformer."[1] It is there to counterbalance the irregularities in the digestive canal in order that they may become regularities in the circulation of the blood. For it would be fatal, especially in one's student days but also at

1 Figure taken from the electrical device which transforms the character of the current.

other times, if certain irregularities in the taking of nutritive matter had necessarily to continue to the full extent of their action into the blood! There is much to be counterbalanced by means of a "backward thrust," as we may call it; only so much is to be conducted over into the blood as is useful to it. This is the function of the spleen, that organ inserted in the blood-stream which so radiates its rhythm-bringing influence over the entire human organism as to produce the condition that has just been described. To external observation, all that we have obtained through the insight of an eye becoming inwardly clairvoyant is evident from the fact that the spleen does keep to a certain rhythm that actually reminds one, even if only slightly, of what I have just been stating. For it is extraordinarily difficult to find out the functions of the spleen by means of external physiological investigation. Outwardly, the only thing that shows itself is that the spleen is to a certain extent inflated for hours at a time after the partaking of a heavy meal; and that, if another meal does not follow, it contracts again.

Here you have a certain expanding and contracting of this organ. When it is realised that the human organism is not what it is often described as being, namely, a mere sum-total of the organs contained within it, but that all the organs send their most secret activities to all parts of the organism, one will then be able also to conceive how the rhythmic movements of the spleen, although dependent, of course, upon the outside world, that is, upon the supply of food, radiate throughout the whole organism and have a counterbalancing influence upon it. Now this is only one of the ways in which the spleen functions. It is impossible to explain all of them at once. Yet it would nevertheless, be extraordinarily interesting, since not everybody is capable of becoming clairvoyant, if such facts could be accepted by external physiology, accepted, let us say, as possible ideas, so that people would say: "I will for once imagine that what is attained by means of the inner clairvoyant eye is, after all, not such complete nonsense as it is often supposed to be. On the contrary, I shall neither believe nor disbelieve this; but I shall let it remain as an idea presented to me, and shall then investigate what external physiology can point out, whether, out of all that is asserted by occultists, anything whatever can be substantiated by showing clearly that it is actually confirmed by external observation."[1]

In a certain sense, what I have just said is such a confirmation. For it has become evident to us that the expansion and contraction of the spleen, due to the inner structure of the organ have a certain regularity; but that, since these movements follow the eating of a meal, they are dependent also on the supply of external nourishment. Thus we have here in the spleen an organ which is dependent from the one aspect, that of the digestive canal, on external, human will; but from the other aspect, that of the blood, we have in it an organ that sets aside to a certain extent human choice, rejects it, and leads back to a rhythm, indeed, we might say, in this way really forms man in accordance with his being. For, if man is to be fashioned in accordance with his being, it is then especially necessary that the central instrument of that being, the blood, should be able to exercise its activity in the right way, in its own blood-rhythm. The human being, in so far as he is the carrier of his own blood-stream, must be set apart, so to speak, within himself, isolated from what proceeds with irregularity in the outside world, that outside world which he incorporates within himself when he takes

1 See in this connection *Physiologischer und physikalischer Nachweis der Wirksamkeit kleinster Entitaeten*. L. Kolisko. Orient-Occident Verlag, Stuttgart, Germany.

in his nourishment out of it. Hence this is a process of isolation, a making the human being independent of the outside world. Every such individualising of any being, making it independent, is called in occultism *saturnine,* something brought about by the Saturn influence. This, as a matter of fact is the original idea associated with Saturn, that from an existing world some sort of Being is isolated, individualised, in such a way that within itself and of itself it can evolve regularity.

I shall for the present disregard the fact that the astronomy of our day reckons both Uranus and Neptune, which are outside the orbit of Saturn, as belonging to our solar system. For the occultist all those forces present in our entire solar system are, for the purpose of isolating them from the rest of the cosmos and individualising them, to be found in the Saturn forces—in that planet therefore, which is the most remote one belonging to this system. If, then, we visualise the entire solar system, we might say: The solar system must be so placed that it can follow its own laws within the orbit of encircling Saturn, and can make itself independent by tearing itself loose, as it were, from the surrounding world and from the formative forces of this surrounding world. For this reason occultists of all the ages have seen in the Saturn forces that which secludes our solar system within itself, thus making it possible for the solar system to develop a rhythm of its own which is not the same as the rhythm outside the world of our solar system.

In a certain way the spleen does something similar within our organism. Certainly we do not in this organism of ours have to do with a separating from the entire outside world, but only with a separating from this surrounding world in so far as it contains the nourishment for our organism and we ourselves introduce its activities into ourselves. The spleen is the organ we first meet when we do this, dealing, so to speak, with everything from outside in the same way as the Saturn forces deal with everything within our solar system, within the orbit of Saturn. The forces that are in the spleen isolate the circulation of our blood from all outside influences, and make of it a regular rhythm within itself, a system having its own rhythm.

Here we have already come nearer, although we are not yet really near as we shall see later, to those reasons, still more or less external, for which such names as the ones already mentioned are chosen in occultism. They are chosen because the occultist does not connect with the names borne by the planets merely what concerns the planets. When these names were originally created in the occult schools they were never applied merely to the separate planets; the name *Saturn,* for instance, was applied to anything that excluded a world outside from a system that took on a rhythmic form within itself. There is always a certain disadvantage for cosmic evolution, as a whole, when one system shuts itself off and regulates itself within itself, fashions a rhythm of its own. And the occultists have, consequently, been somewhat concerned about this disadvantage. We might say, indeed, that it is quite comprehensible that all activities in the entire universe have a basic inner relation and are mutually related. If any one "world," be it a solar system, or be it the blood-system of the human being, is completely separated from the the rest of the universe surrounding it, this signifies that it quite independently violates external laws, makes itself independent of them, changes itself and creates its own inner laws, its own rhythm. We shall see later how this may also be true in the case of the human being although it must be clear to us, in view of the whole discussion in to-day's lecture, that it is mostly a blessing that man maintains this inner Saturn-rhythm which the spleen has created for him. At the same time we shall see that we can apply this law also in the case of man, namely, that any being, whether it be a planet or a man, brings itself through seclusion within itself into a state of contradiction to the world around it. A contradiction is thus created between that which surrounds and that which is within the being concerned. this contradiction cannot be compensated for, after it has once appeared, until the inner rhythm set up has again adapted itself completely to the outer rhythm. We shall see that this apples also to the human being; for otherwise, according to what has been said, he would be compelled to adapt himself to irregularity. We shall find, however, that such is not the case. The inner rhythm, although it has established itself, must again strive after doing this to fashion itself in accordance with the entire outside world, which means that it must eliminate itself. Thus the being first comes to have an inner existence of its own; but, because it can now work independently, it aspires to adapt itself to the outside world and to become harmonious with it. To put it in other words, everything that has made itself independent as a result of a saturnine activity is doomed at the same time, because of this saturnine activity, to destroy itself again. Saturn, or Kronos, devours his own children, so the myth tells us. Here you see a deeply significant harmony between an occult idea, expressed in the name *Kronos* or *Saturn*, and a myth which expresses the same thing in a picture, a symbol: "Kronos devours his own children!"

We can try, at least, to let such things work upon us; and, if we allow them to do so in ever-increasing number, one new fact after another comes to light till it becomes impossible after a time to say, in the light and easy manner in which we so often hear a superficial solution proposed: "Here are some of these visionaries dreaming that the old myths and sagas contained the pictorial impress of a deeper wisdom!" If a man hears two or three, or let us say even ten, such "correspondences" presented, as these so often are presented in literature in a wholly superficial way, it is of course quite possible for him to oppose the idea that there is a deeper wisdom contained in the myths and sagas than in external science; that mythology leads us deeper into the foundations of things and of Being than do the methods of natural-scientific study. But if he allows such examples to work upon him again and again, and then becomes aware that, throughout the whole extent of the thought and feeling of men and of peoples, it is verified that in pictorial conceptions everywhere and always, over all parts of the earth, anyone with a very accurate observation and devoted interest in sagas and myths may find the metamorphoses of a deeper wisdom, then he will be able to understand why certain occultists can with justice say as they do: "He alone really comprehends the myths and sagas who has penetrated into human nature with the help of occult physiology." And, indeed, more truly than is the case in external science do even the names in these myths and sagas and other traditions contain real physiology. When once people begin to fathom how much physiology was coined, for instance, in such names as *Cain* and *Abel,* and into the names of all their successors in those olden days when it was customary to coin an inner meaning into names, when they once see how much physiology, how much inner understanding for homely human wisdom is contained in those old names in a truly remarkable way, they will then win a tremendous respect and the deepest reverence for everything that has been devised in the course of the historical evolution of man for the purpose of enabling the soul, where it cannot as yet through its own wisdom ascend into the spiritual world, to have a conscious inner experience by means of *pictures* of its connection with these spiritual worlds. Then will be completely banished that idea which plays too large a part at the present time: "What splendid progress we men of to-day have made!" by which is often also meant: "How well we have succeeded in getting rid of those old pictorial expressions belonging to prehistoric 'wisdom'!" We shall then cast away such feelings, and immerse ourselves with whole-hearted devotion in the course of human evolution throughout its successive epochs. For what the clairvoyant, with his opened inner eye, establishes physiologically as the inner nature of the human organs, is so expressed in these ancient pictures that the myths and sagas really contain in them the truth of the origin of man. To make possible the expression in pictures of this miraculous process, whereby external worlds have been compressed into human organs and have condensed and crystallised themselves in the course of infinitely long periods of time in order that they might become something which, in the form of a spleen for example, brings about an inner rhythm within us, or in the form of a liver or gall-bladder, etc., as we shall see to-morrow—to be able to express all this in pictures requires a divining of what we can rediscover by means of occult science about the human organisation. For what we find there has been born out of the worlds, as a microcosm out of the macrocosm. We look into this whole origin or beginning with the help of occult science on the one hand; and we see on the other that intimations of these beginnings are contained in the myths and sagas, and that those occultists are right who find a real meaning in them only when they are given a *physiological* foundation.

It is our purpose to-day at least to indicate these facts, if no more; for this can help us to win that reverence of which we spoke in our first hours together. If we practise such a method of study as this, quite apart now from the "pictures" belonging to the different peoples, by also directly pointing to what presents itself to a deeper investigation of the spiritual content of the human organs, if we are able to present this even only to a very limited extent, it will soon become clear to us what a miraculous structure this human organism is. In this series of lectures we shall endeavour to throw a little light upon the inner quality of being of this human organism.

MAN'S INNER COSMIC SYSTEM

23rd March, 1911.

Our discussion of yesterday, dealing primarily with the significance of one of those organs which represent an "inner cosmic system" of man, will be continued to-day. We shall then find the transition leading to a description of the functions of the other human organs and organ-systems.

It was said to me yesterday in connection with my reference to the spleen that there might arise an apparent contradiction as regards the very important function ascribed to the spleen in the entire being of man; that this contradiction might well appear as a result of the reflection that it is possible to take the spleen out of the body, actually to remove it, and yet not leave the man incapable of living.

Such an objection is certainly justified from the standpoint of our contemporaries; indeed, it is unavoidable in view of the fact that certain difficulties present themselves even to those who approach the spiritual-scientific world-conception as thoroughly honest seekers. It was possible to point out only in a general way in our first public lecture[1] how our contemporaries, especially when conscientiously schooled in scientific methods, find difficulties as soon as they choose the road that leads them to an understanding of what may be presented out of the occult depths of cosmic Being.

Now, we shall see in the course of these lectures how, in

[1] Single lecture delivered on 19th March 1911. Not available in English translation.

principle, so to speak, such an objection gradually disappears of itself. Today however I shall draw your attention in a preliminary way to the fact that the removal of the spleen from the human organism is thoroughly compatible with everything discussed yesterday. If we really wish to ascend to the truths of spiritual science, we must accustom ourselves gradually to the fact that what we call the human organism, as seen by means of our external senses, and also everything we see in this organism as substance, or it might, perhaps, be better to say as external matter, that all this is not the *whole* man; but that, underlying man as a physical organism (as we shall explain further) are higher, supersensible human organisms called the ether-body or life-body, the astral body and the ego; and that we have in this physical organism only the external physical expression for the corresponding formation and processes of the ether-body, the astral body, etc.

When we refer to an organ such as the spleen we think of it in the spiritual-scientific sense, realising that not only does something take place in the external, physical spleen, but that this is merely the physical expression for corresponding processes which take place in the ether-body, for example, or in the astral body. We might say moreover, that the more any one of the organs is the direct expression of the spiritual, the less is the physical form of the organ, that is, what we have before us as physical substance, the determining factor. Just as we find in looking at a pendulum that its movement is merely the physical expression of gravity, even so is the physical organ merely the physical expression of the supersensible influences working in force and form—with this difference, however, that in the case of such forces as that of gravitation when we remove the pendulum, which is the physical expression, no inner rhythm due to gravitation can continue. This is the case, of course, in inanimate, inorganic

Nature; but not in the same way in animate, organic Nature. When there are no other causes present in the organism as a whole it is not necessary that the spiritual influences should cease with the removal of the physical organ; for this physical organ, in its physical nature, is only a feeble expression of the nature of the corresponding spiritual activities. On this point we shall have more to say later.

Accordingly when we observe the human being, with reference to his spleen, we have to do in the first place, with that organ only; but beyond that with a system of forces working in it which have in the physical spleen only their outward expression. If one removes the spleen, these forces which are integral parts of the organism still continue to work. Their activities do not cease in the way in which, let us say, certain spiritual activities in the human being cease when one removes the brain or a portion of it. It may even be, under certain circumstances, that an organ which has become diseased may cause a much greater hindrance to the continuation of the spiritual activities that is brought about by the removal of the organ concerned. This is true, for example, in the case of a serious disease of the spleen. If it is possible to remove the organ when it becomes seriously diseased, this removal is, under certain conditions, less hindering to the development of the spiritual activities than is the organ itself, which is inwardly diseased and therefore a constant mischief-maker, opposing the development of the underlying spiritual forces.

Such an objection a man may make if he has not yet penetrated very deeply into the real nature of spiritual-scientific knowledge. Though readily understood, this is one of those objections that disappear of themselves when one has time and patience to go more deeply into these matters. You will generally find the following to be true: When anyone approaches what is given out through spiritual science with a certain sort of knowledge gathered from all that belongs to present-day science, contradiction after contradiction may result till finally one can get no further. And, if a man is quick to form opinions, he will certainly not be able to reach any other conclusion than that spiritual science is a sort of madness which does not harmonise in the slightest degree with the results obtained by external science. If, however, a man follows these things with patience, he will see that there is no contradiction, not even of the most minute kind, between what comes forth from spiritual science and what may be presented by external science. The difficulty before us is this, that the field of anthroposophical or spiritual science as a whole is so extensive that it is never possible to present more than a part of it. When people approach such parts they may feel discrepancies such as that which we have described; yet it would be impossible to begin in any other way than this with the much needed bringing of the anthroposophical world-conception into the culture and knowledge of our day.

Yesterday I endeavoured to explain the transformation of rhythm, in the sense I explained, which is undertaken by the spleen in contrast to the rhythmless manner in which human beings take their external nourishment. I took what was said in this connection as my point of departure because it is in itself fundamentally the most easily understood of all the functions belonging to the spleen. We must know, however, that although it is the easiest to understand it is not the most important, it does not constitute the chief thing. For, if it were, people could always say: "Very well, then; if the human being were to take pains to know the right rhythm for his nourishment, the activity of the spleen viewed from this aspect would little by little become unnecessary. From this we see at once that what was described yesterday is the merest trifle. Far more important is the fact that in the process of nourishment we have to do with external substances, external articles of food, their composition and the form and manner in which they exist in our environment. So long as one holds to the conception that these nutritive substances are so much dead bulk, or at best masses containing that sort of life which one generally assumes to be in plants and other articles of food, it may certainly appear as if all that is necessary is for the external substances taken into the organism as nutritive matter to be simply worked over by means of what we call the process of digestion in its broadest sense.

Many people, it is true, imagine that they have to do with some sort of indeterminate substance taken in as food, a substance quite neutral in its relation to us which simply waits, when we have once taken it in, till we are able to digest it. But such is not the case. Articles of food are, after all not just bricks which serve in some sort of way as building material for the construction they are to help in erecting. Bricks are included in the architect's plan in any way he pleases to use them because they represent in relationship to the building a mass in itself quite inert. This is not true, however, of nutritive matter in its relation to the human being. For every particle of substance we have in our environment has certain inner forces, its own conformity to law. This is the essential element in any substance that it has its own inner activities. Accordingly, when we bring external nutritive substances into our organism, when we insert them into our own inner activity, so to speak, they do not simply consent to this at once as a matter of course but attempt first to develop their own laws, their own rhythms and their own inner forms of movement.

Thus, if the human organism wishes to use these substances

for its own purposes it must first destroy their rhythmic life, as it were, that vital activity which is peculiarly their own. It must do away with these, not merely working over some indifferent material, but working in opposition to certain laws characteristic of these substances. That these substances do have their own laws can soon be felt by the human being when, for instance, a strong poison is conveyed through the digestive canal. He soon feels, in such a case, that the particular law belonging to this substance has mastered him, that these laws now assert themselves. Just as every poison has in general its own inner laws by means of which it carries out an attack on our organism, so it is with every substance, with all the nutriment that we take in. It is not something neutral, but rather it asserts itself in accordance with its own nature, its own quality of being. It has, we may say, its own rhythm. This rhythm must be combated by the human being, so that it is not only a case of working over neutral building material within man's inner organisation, but rather that the peculiar nature of this building material must first be mastered.

We may say, therefore, that in those organs which our food first encounters inside the human being we have the instruments with which to oppose in the first place, what constitutes the peculiar life of the nutritive substances—"life" here to be conceived in its wider meaning, so that even the apparently lifeless world of nature, with its laws of movement, is included. That which the food has within it as its own rhythm, which contradicts the human rhythm, must be modified. And in this work of change the organism of the spleen is, so to speak, the outpost. In this changing of the rhythm, however, in this work of re-forming and of defending, the other organs we have mentioned also participate; so that in the spleen, the gall-bladder, and the liver we have a co-operating system of organs whose main function it is, when food is received into the organism, to repel what constitutes the particular inner nature of this food. All the activity first developed in the stomach, or even before the food reaches it, and everything which is then brought about by the secretion[1] of the gall, and which takes place further through the activity of the liver and the spleen, all of this results in that warding off we have mentioned of the peculiar nature of the nutritive substances.

Thus our food is adapted, we may say, to the inner rhythm of the human organism only when it has been met by the counter-activity of these organs. Only, therefore, when we have taken in our nutriment, and have exposed it to the activity of these organs, do we have in us something capable of being received into that organic system which is the bearer, the instrument, of our ego. Before any sort of external nutritive substance can be received into this blood of ours, so that the blood shall become capable of serving as the instrument of our ego, all those forms of law peculiar to the external world must be set aside, and the blood must receive the nutriment in such form as corresponds to the particular nature of the human organism. We may say, therefore, that in the spleen, the liver and the gall-bladder as they are in themselves and as they react upon the stomach, we have those organs which adapt the laws of the outside world, from which we take our food, to the inner organisation, the inner rhythm, of man.

This human nature, however, in all its working as a totality and with all its members, confronts not only the inner world; it must also be in a continual correspondence or intercourse with the outside world, in a continual living reciprocal activity in relation to that world. This living interaction with the

1 For a fuller explanation of the terms translated in these Lectures as *secretion* and *excretion*, see note on p. 103.

world outside is cut off by the fact that, in so far as we come into connection with it through our nutritive material, the three organ-systems of the liver, the gall-bladder, and the spleen are placed in opposition to the laws of that world. From this side, through these organs, conformity to external law is eliminated. If the human organism were exposed only to these systems of organs it would shut itself off completely so to speak, from the outside world, would itself become, as a system of organs, an entity completely isolated in itself. Something else, therefore, is necessary. Just as the human being needs, on the one hand, organ-systems by means of which the outside world is so reshaped as to be in accordance with his inner world, so must he be in a position also, on the other hand, to confront the outside world directly with the help of the instrument of his ego: that is, he must place his organism, which otherwise would remain a kind of entity isolated within itself, in direct continual connection with the outside world.

Whereas the blood enters into connection with the external world from the one direction, only in such a way that it contains that part of this world alone from which all forms of law peculiar to it have been cast aside from the other side it enters into relation with this external world so that it can in a certain sense come into direct contact with it. This happens when the blood flows through the lungs and comes into contact with the outer air. It is there renewed by means of the oxygen in this outer air, and is brought into such a form that nothing can now weaken it in this form; so that the oxygen of the air thus actually meets the instrument of the human ego in a condition that conforms with its own essential nature and quality of being.

There appears thus before our eyes this truly remarkable fact: that what we may call the noblest instrument possessed by man, his blood, which is the instrument of his ego, stands there as an entity that receives all its nourishment, everything that it takes from the life of the outside world, carefully filtered by the organ-systems we have characterised. In this way the blood is made capable of becoming a complete expression of the inner organisation of man, the inner rhythm of man. On the other hand, however, in so far as the blood comes into direct contact with the outside world, with that particular substance in the external world that may be taken in as it is, in its own inner form of law, its own vital activity, without needing to be directly combated, to that extent is this human organism not something secluded within itself but at the same time in full contact with the world outside.

We have, accordingly, in this blood-organism of man, looked at from this standpoint, something very wonderful. We have in it an actual, genuine means of expression of the human ego, which is in fact turned toward the external world on the one side, and on the other toward its own inner life. Just as man is directed through his nerve-system, as we have seen, toward the impressions of this outer world, taking the outer world into himself, as it were, through the nerves by way of the soul, just so does he come into direct contact with the outer world through the instrument of his blood, in that the blood receives oxygen from the air through the lungs. We may say, therefore, that in the system of the spleen, liver, and gall-bladder, on the one hand, and in the lung-system on the other, we have two systems which counteract each other. Outer world and inner world, so to speak, have an absolutely direct contact with each other in the human organism by means of the blood, because the blood comes into contact on the one side with the outer air and on the other with the nutritive material that has been deprived of its own nature. One might say that the forces of the two worlds come into collision within man, like positive and negative electricity. We can very easily picture to ourselves where the organ-system is located which is designed to permit the collision of these two systems of cosmic forces to have an effect upon it. The transformed nutritive juices work upward as far as the heart, inasmuch as the blood which carries them streams through the heart; the oxygen of the air which enters the blood directly from the outer world works inward to the heart, inasmuch as the blood flows through it. In the heart therefore we have that organ in which these two systems into which the human being is interwoven to which he is attached from two different directions meet each other. The whole *inner* organism of man is joined to the heart on the one side, and on the other, this inner organism itself is connected directly through the heart with the rhythm, the inner vital activity, of the *outer* world.

It is quite possible that when two such systems collide the direct result of their interaction may be a harmony. The system of the great outside world or macrocosm presses upon us through the fact that it sends the oxygen or the air in general into our inner organism, and the system of our small inner world or microcosm transforms our nourishment; therefore we might imagine that these systems, because of the fact that the blood streams through the heart, are able in the blood to create a harmonious balance. If this *were* so, the human being would be yoked to two worlds, so to speak, providing him with his inner equilibrium. Now, we shall see later in the course of these lectures, that the connection between the world and the human being is not such that the world leaves us quite passive—that it sends its forces into us in two different ways, while we are simply harnessed to their counteracting influences. No, it is not like that; but rather, as we shall more and more learn to know, the essential thing with regard to man is the fact that at last a residue always remains for his own inner activity; and that it is left ultimately to man himself to bring about the balance, the inner equilibrium, right into his very organs. We must, therefore, seek within the human organism itself for the balancing of these two world-systems, the harmonising of these two systems of organs. We must realise that the harmonising of these two organ-systems is not already provided through that kind of conformity to law operating outside man and that other kind of conformity to law which works only within his own organism, but that this must be evoked through the help of an organ-system of his own. Man must establish the harmony within himself. (We are not now speaking of the consciousness, but of those processes which take place entirely unconsciously within the organ-systems of the human being.) This balancing of the two systems, the system of spleen, liver, gall-bladder on the one hand and the lung-system on the other, as they confront the blood which flows through the heart is, indeed, brought about. It is brought about through the fact that we have the *kidney-system* inserted in the entire human organism and in intimate relationship with the circulation of the blood.

In this kidney-system we have that which harmonises, as it were, the outer activities due to the direct contact of the blood with the air and those other activities proceeding from the inner human organism itself in that the food must first be prepared by being deprived of its own nature. In this kidney-system, accordingly, we have a balancing system between the two kinds of organ-systems previously characterised; and the organism is in a position by means of this system to dispose of the excess which otherwise would result from the inharmonious interaction of the two other systems.

Over against the entire inner organisation, the organs

belonging to the digestive apparatus (in which we must include the organs we have learned to know as liver, gall-bladder, and spleen), we have placed that system for which these organs primarily develop their preparatory activity, namely, the blood-system. But also over against this blood-system we have placed those organs which work, on the one hand to counteract a one-sided isolation, but on the other hand to create a balance between the inner systems we have mentioned and what presses inward from without. If we think, therefore, of the blood-system with its central point, the heart, as placed in the middle of the organism—and we shall see how truly justifiable this is—we have adjoining this system of blood and heart, on the one side the spleen, liver, and gall-bladder systems, and connected with it on the other side the lung and kidney systems. We shall emphasise later on how extremely interesting this connection is between the lung-system and the kidney-system. If we sketch the systems side by side we have in them everything belonging to the inner organisation of man which is

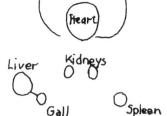

related in a special way, and which so presents itself to us in this relationship that we are obliged to look upon the heart, together with the blood-system belonging to it, as by far the most important part. Now, I have already pointed out, and we shall see even more definitely to what an extent such a giving of names as we have described is justified, that in occultism the activity of the spleen is characterised as a Saturn-activity, that of the liver as a Jupiter-activity, and that of the gall-bladder as a Mars-activity. On the same basis on which these names were chosen for the activities here

referred to, occult knowledge
sees in the heart and the blood-
system belonging to it something
in the human organism which
merits the name Sun, just as the
sun outside merits this name in
the planetary system. In the
lung-system, there is contained
what the occultists, according

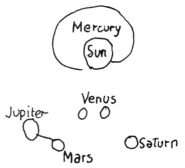

to the same principle, characterise as *Mercury*, and in the
kidney-system that which merits the name *Venus*. Thus, by
means of these names, we have pointed out in these systems
of the human organism, even if at the present moment we do
not in the least undertake a justification of the names, something like an *inner world* system. We have, moreover, sup-
plemented this inner world system in that we have placed
ourselves in a position to observe the relationship which
manifests itself in the very nature of man as holding good for
the two other organ-systems having a certain special connection with the blood-system. Only when we observe these
things in such a way do we present something complete in
respect to what we may call the real inner human world.
In the following lectures I shall have occasion to show you
that the occultists have actual reasons for conceiving the
relationship of the sun to Mercury and Venus as being similar
to that which we must necessarily think of as existing
between the heart and lungs and kidneys respectively, within
the human organism.

We see, therefore, that in the instrument of our ego, our
blood-system, expressing its rhythm in the heart, something
is present that is determined to a certain extent in its entire
formation, its inner nature and quality of being, by man's
inner world system; something that must first be embedded

in the inner world system of the human being before it can live as it actually does live. We have in this human blood-system, as I have often stated, the physical instrument of our ego. Indeed, we know that our ego as constituted is only possible by reason of the fact that it is built up on the foundation of a physical body, an ether-body, and an astral body. An ego free to fly about in the world by itself, as a human ego, is unthinkable. A human ego within this world, which is the world that for the moment concerns us, pre-supposes as its basis an astral body, an ether-body, and a physical body.

Now, just as this ego in its spiritual connection presupposes the three members of man's being we have just named, so does its physical organ, the blood-system, which is the instrument of the ego, presuppose likewise on the physical side corresponding images, as it were, of the astral body and the ether-body. Thus the blood-system can carry out its evolution only on the basis of something else. Whereas the plant simply evolves out of inanimate and inorganic nature, in that it grows directly out of this, we must say that in the case of the human blood-organism the mere outer world cannot serve as a basis in the way that it serves the plant, but this outer world must first be transformed by way of our nutrition. And just as the physical body of man must bear within itself the ether-body and the astral body, so what streams in with the food must first be transformed before that which is the instrument of the human ego can merge itself with these transformed nutritive substances.

Even though we may say that the nature of this physical organ, this physical instrument of the human ego, is de-termined in the lung-system by the outer world, it is never-theless so determined by the outer world that it is, after all, an organ of the human bodily organisation. Here again we must differentiate between what comes to man from outside in the form of air (is breathed in and enables him to permeate his blood directly with the rhythm belonging to the outer world) and what approaches the blood, the living instrument of the ego in the organism, not directly, but, as has already been described, by the roundabout path of the soul: everything, namely, that man takes in by receiving the impressions of the outer world through the senses, so that the senses then convey these impressions to the tablet of the blood.

We may, therefore, state it thus: Not only does man come by means of the air into direct physical contact with the outside world, in that this contact works right into his blood; but by means of the sense organs he also comes into contact with the outside world in such a way that this contact is a non-physical one, taking place through the process of perception which the soul unfolds when it comes into relation with its environment.

We here have something like a higher process in addition to the process of breathing, something like a spiritualised breathing process. Whereas through the breathing process we take the outer world in the form of matter into our organism, we take, through the process of perception, by which I mean here everything that we work over inwardly in connection with the external impressions we receive, something into our organism which is a spiritualised process of breathing. And there now arises the question: "How do these two processes work together?" For in the human organism everything must have a reciprocal, a counterbalancing activity. Let us for a moment put this question still more exactly, for certain essential things will depend upon an accurate presentation.

In order to be able to convey to our minds the answer

which we shall give to-day hypothetically, we must first understand clearly how an interaction, a reciprocal activity, can take place between all that works through the blood, all that the blood has changed into through the fact that the different processes have come about under the influence of the inner world system, and what we carry on as processes of external perception. For, in spite of the fact that the blood is thus filtered, and even though so much care has been taken to make it the wonderfully organised substance it is, so that it can be the instrument of our ego, in spite of this it is nevertheless primarily a physical substance in the human organism, and belongs as such to the physical body. At first, therefore, there seems to be a very great difference between this human blood, which has been prepared as it has, and what we know as our processes of perception, everything, that is, which the soul performs. Indeed, this is an undeniable *reality*, for anyone would have to be remarkably lacking in ability to think, who would deny that perceptions, concepts, feelings, and will-impulses *exist* just the same as does a blood-substance, a nerve-substance, a liver-substance, a gall-substance. As to *how* these things are connected world-conceptions might begin to conflict. They might dispute, let us say, as to whether thoughts are merely some sort of activity of the nerve-substance, or something of that sort. It is only at this point that the conflict can begin between the different world-conceptions. No world-conception can dispute over the obvious fact that our inner soul-life, our thought-life, our feeling-life, everything which builds itself up on the foundation of external perceptions and impressions, presents a reality in itself. Note well that I did not say, in the first place, "an absolutely isolated reality," but "a reality in *itself*," for nothing in the world is isolated. The words "reality in itself" are intended to indicate what may be observed as being real within our inner world system; and to this last belong all our thoughts, feelings and so forth, quite as truly as do the stomach, the liver, and the gall-bladder.

Yet something else may strike us when we see these two realities side by side—everything on the one hand which, even though so thoroughly filtered, is none the less physical, namely, the blood; and on the other hand that which at first appears, indeed, to have nothing at all to do with anything physical, namely, the content of the soul-life, consisting of feelings, thoughts and so forth. As a matter of fact this very aspect of these two kinds of reality presents man with such difficulties that the most varied answers, offered by the most diverse world-conceptions, have come to be associated with it.

There are world-conceptions, for instance, that believe in a direct influence upon physical substance of everything connected with the soul, with thought and with feeling, as if thought could work directly upon physical substance. In contrast to these, there are others which assume that thoughts, feelings, and so forth, are simply the products of the processes that take place in physical substance. The dispute between these two world-conceptions has through long periods of time played an important rôle in the outside world, but not in the field of occultism, in which it is considered a dispute over empty words.

Since no ultimate agreement was reached, there has appeared during more recent times still another conception bearing the strange name of "psycho-physical parallelism." If I were to express it rather trivially I might say that since the disputants had no longer any other resource, not knowing whether spirit works upon the processes of the physical body or whether these bodily processes influence the spirit, they concluded that there are two processes running parallel courses. They argued: at the same time that man thinks, feels and so forth, certain definite parallel processes are taking place in his physical organism. The perception, "I see red," would according to this correspond to some sort of material process. But they do not go any further than to say that it "corresponds." Indeed, this is a mere expedient which leads them out of all their difficulties, but only in the sense that it sets these aside, not that it overcomes them. All the disputes that have arisen on this basis, including the futility of the psycho-physical parallelism, result from the fact that people insist upon deciding these questions on a basis upon which they simply cannot be decided. We have to do with non-material processes when we consider the activities of our soul-life as inner life; and we have to do with material processes when we centre our attention upon the blood, the most highly organised thing in us. If we simply compare these two things, physical activities and soul-activities, and then seek by means of reflection to find out how each of them works upon the other, we shall not arrive anywhere. Through reflection one may find all sorts of arbitrary solution or non-solutions. The only way to determine anything in regard to these questions is actually to establish a higher knowledge. This does not limit itself either to viewing the outer world with the physical senses or to thought that is bound up with a merely physical external world, but elevates itself to a certain extent to what leads beyond the physical, and likewise to that which leads into the super-physical world from our own inner soul-life which indeed we experience in the physical world. We must ascend, on the one hand, from the material to the supersensible, the super-material. On the other hand, we must ascend also from our soul-life to the super-physical, that is, to that which lies at the basis of our soul-life in the super-physical world; for our soul-life, with all its feelings, etc., is, of course, something that we experience in the physical world. We must, accordingly, ascend from both sides to a super-physical world.

Now, in order to ascend from the material side to the super-physical world, those soul-exercises are necessary which enable man to look behind the external, the sensible, behind that veil, of which I spoke yesterday, into which are woven our sense-impressions. Moreover, such sense-impressions as these we also have before us, of course, when we observe the whole external organism of man. And when we descend to the very finest element of the human organism, to the blood, we are, nevertheless, dealing with a merely physical-sensible thing when we observe it, at first, with the physical senses, or at least with the instruments and methods of external science, which give us just such a picture of the blood as would an external eye if it could see this blood directly.

We have said, then, that with the help of such soul-exercise as lead up into the supersensible world, we can penetrate into the foundations of the physical world, into the super-sensible element in the human organism. In doing this, the first supersensible thing we meet in this human organism is what we call the *ether-body*. This ether-body (and we shall describe it still more accurately from the standpoint of occult physiology) is a super-sensible organisation, which we first think of simply as the supersensible basic substance out of which the sensible or physical organism of man is constructed, and of which it is a copy. Of course the blood is also an impress or copy of this ether-body. Thus we have already at this point, by coming only one stage beyond the sense-organism, something supersensible in the human ether-body, and the question now arises: are we able to approach this supersensible also from the other side, from the side of the soul-life, from what we experience in the sensations, thoughts and feelings that we build up on the basis of our impressions of the outside world?

We have already seen that we cannot approach the physical organism directly, for the physical and material place themselves in our way. Can we approach the ether-organism? It is clear that we cannot approach it as directly as we can our soul-life. When we are at work in our soul what at first happens is that we receive external impressions. The outside world acts upon our senses, and we then work over the external impressions in our soul. But we do more than that, we store up, so to speak, these impressions which we have received. Just think for a moment about the simple phenomenon of memory, when you recall something that you experienced, perhaps years ago. At that time, on the basis of external perceptions, certain impressions took form, which you then worked over, and which you draw up to-day out of the depths of your soul, and to-day there comes to you the memory of a tree, let us say, or an odour. Here you have stored up something in your soul which could remain yours from the external impression and the elaboration of it in your soul, something that can form in you the recollection.

We now find, however, through observation of the soul-life attained through exercises of the soul, that in the moment when we have developed our soul-life far enough to be able to store up mental pictures in the memory we are not working with our soul experiences only in our ego. We first confront the outside world with our ego, take impressions from it into our ego, and work these over in our astral body. But, were we to work them over only in the astral body, we should straightway forget them. When we draw conclusions we are at work in our astral bodies; but when we fix impressions within us so firmly that, after some little time has passed, or indeed after only a few minutes, we can again recall them, we have impressed upon our ether-body these impressions received through our ego and worked over in our astral body. In these memory-pictures, accordingly, we have drawn out of our ego down into our ether-body that which we have lived over inwardly as activity of soul in our contact with the outer world. Now, if we have something which impresses upon the ether-body our memory-pictures taken, as it were, from the soul, and if from the other side we recognise the ether-body as that super-sensible expression of our organism which is nearest to the physical, the question then arises: *How* does this imprinting come about? In other words, when the human being works over external impressions, makes them into memory-pictures, and in doing so thrusts them into his ether-body, how does it happen that he does actually bring down into the ether-body what the astral body has first worked over and what now presses against the ether-body? How does he transfer it?

This transfer takes place in a very remarkable way. If we observe the blood—let us now imagine ourselves within the human ether-body—quite schematically as it courses through the heart, and think of it as the external physical expression of the human ego, we thereby see how this ego works, how it receives impressions corresponding with the outer world and condenses these to memory-pictures. We see, further-more, not only that our blood is active in this process, but also that, throughout its course, especially in the upward direction, somewhat less in the downward, it stirs up the ether-body, so that we see currents developing everywhere in the ether-body, taking a very definite course, as if they would join the blood flowing upward from the heart and go up to the head. And in the head these currents come together, in about the same way, to use a comparison belonging to the external world, as do currents of electricity when they rush toward a point which is opposed by another point, so as to neutralise the positive and the negative. When we observe with a soul trained in occult methods, we see at this point ether-forces compressed as if under a very powerful tension, those ether-forces which are called forth through the impressions that now desire to become definite concepts, memory-pictures, and to stamp themselves upon the ether-body.

I shall, therefore, draw here the last out-streamings of these ether-currents, as they flow up toward the brain, and show their crowding together somewhat as this would actually appear. We see here a very powerful tension which concentrates at one point, and announces: "I will now enter into the ether-body!" just as when positive and negative electricity are impelled to neutralise each other. We then see  how, in opposition to these, other currents flow from that portion of the ether-body which belongs to the rest of the bodily organisation. These currents go out for the most part from the lower part of the breast, but also from the lymph vessels and other organs, and come together in such a way that they oppose these other currents. Thus we have in the brain, whenever a memory-picture wishes to form itself, two ether-currents, one coming from below and one from above, which oppose each other under the greatest possible tension, just as two electric currents oppose each other. If a balance is brought about between these two currents, then a concept has become a memory-picture and has incorporated itself in the ether-body.

Such supersensible currents in the human organism always express themselves by creating for themselves also a physical material-organ, which we must first regard as a materialisation. Thus we have within us an organ, situated in the mid brain, which is the physical material-expression for that which wishes to take the form of a memory-picture; and opposite to this is situated still another organ in the brain. These two organs in the human brain are the physical-material expression of the two currents in the human ether-body; they are, one might say, something like the ultimate indication of the fact that there are such currents in the ether-body. These currents condense themselves with such force that they seize the human bodily substance and consolidate it into these organs. We thus actually get an impression of bright etheric light-currents streaming across from the one to the other of these organs, and pouring themselves out over the human ether-body. These organs are

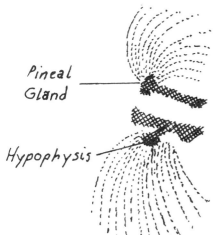

Pineal Gland

Hypophysis

actually present in the human organism. One of them is the *pineal gland*; the other, the so-called *pituitary body*: the "epiphysis" and the "hypophysis" respectively. We have here, at a definite point in the human physical organism, the external physical expression of the co-operation of soul and body!

This is what I wished in the first place to give you by way of general principles. With this we conclude to-day's lecture, and to-morrow we will continue our discussion further and find yet more to add to it. It is always important to hold firmly and clearly to the thought that we can always investigate the supersensible, and can ask ourselves whether the physical expression of the supersensible world that we should expect to find is actually present. We see here that these sense-expressions of the supersensible actually do exist. Since we have here, however, a question of an entrance gate from the sense-world to the supersensible, you will understand that these two organs are in the highest degree puzzling to physical science, and you will, therefore, be able to get from external science only inadequate information with regard to them.

THE SYSTEMS OF SUPERSENSIBLE FORCES

24th March, 1911.

It will be my task to-day, before we continue our studies, to present certain concepts which we shall need to use in the further development of our discussions. In this connection it will be especially important for us to come to an understanding as regards the meaning of that which we call in a spiritual-scientific, anthroposophical sense, a "physical organ," or rather the "physical expression of an organ." For you have already seen that we have a right to say with regard to the spleen, for example, that, as something material, the physical spleen may even be removed or become useless without thereby causing the activity of what we call "the spleen" in the anthroposophical sense to be eliminated. We must say, then, that when we have actually removed a physical organ such as this, there still remains in the organism the inner vital activity which should be carried on by the organ. From this we already see, and I beg you most earnestly to adopt this concept for all that follows, that we can think away, as it were, everything physically visible and perceptible in an organ such as this (it is not possible in the case of every organ) and yet there still remains the functioning, the activity of the organ, with the result that we must consider what then remains as belonging to what is supersensible in the human organism. But, on the other hand, when we speak on the basis of our spiritual science about such organs as the spleen, the liver, the gall-bladder, the kidneys, the lungs, and the like, we are by no means referring when using these names, to what we can see physically, but rather to systems of forces that are in reality of a super-sensible nature. For this reason, precisely in the case of such an organ as the spleen we must think, to begin with, when we speak about it from the spiritual-scientific standpoint, of a system of forces not physically visible to external sight.

Let us then, in the first sketch that I shall draw here, think of a system of forces not physically visible. This would represent a system visible only to supersensible vision; and a system such as that in the region of the spleen, for example, would be visible only as a supersensible system of forces. Now if we bear in mind that, in the actual human organism which we have directly before us, this supersensible system of forces is filled out with physical matter, we must ask ourselves how we shall have to think of the relationship between it and that which is sense-perceptible matter.

I am sure it will not be difficult for you to believe that forces not visible to the senses can traverse space. One need only recall, for example, the following: Anyone who had never heard anything about the reality of air in a bottle would be rather surprised if we were to place an empty bottle on a table and tightly insert a funnel in it, when, on pouring water quickly into the funnel the water in the funnel is held there and cannot flow down into the bottle because the latter contains air. He would then become aware of the fact that there is, indeed, in the bottle something invisible to him which holds back the water. If we imagine this concept carried somewhat further, it will not be difficult to think that space around us may likewise be completely filled with systems of forces which are obviously of a supersensible nature, moreover, of such a supersensible nature that not only can we not cut through them with a knife, but that

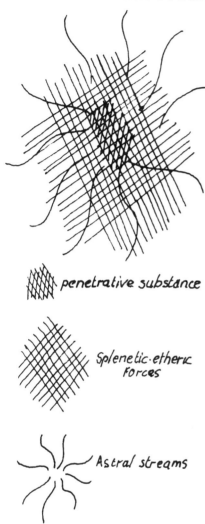

penetrative substance

Splenetic·etheric forces

Astral streams

they cannot be affected when any physical matter such as the kidneys, embedded within these systems of forces, becomes diseased. We must realise, therefore, that the relation between a supersensible system of forces of this sort and what we see as a physical-sensible organ is such that physical matter, belonging to the physical world fits itself in and, attracted by the force-centres, deposits itself within the lines of force. Through the inclusion of physical matter in the supersensible system of forces the organ becomes a physical thing. We may say, therefore, that the reason why, for instance, a physical-sensible organ is visible at the place where the spleen is located is that, at this point, space is filled in a certain definite manner by systems of forces which attract the material substance in such a way that this deposits itself in the form in which we see it in the external organ of the spleen when we study it anatomically.

So you may think that all these diverse organs in the

human organism as being first planned as supersensible organs, and then, under the influence of the most varied sorts of supersensible systems of forces, as being filled with physical matter. Hence, in these force-systems which at different points of the organism deposit physical matter within themselves, we must recognise a supersensible organism which is differentiated within itself and which incorporates physical matter within itself in the most diverse ways. We have thus obtained, not only this one concept of the relationships of the supersensible systems of forces to the physical matter deposited in the organs, but also the other concept of the process of nourishing the organism as a whole. For this process of nourishing the entire organism consists in nothing else, after all, than in so preparing the nutritive substances taken in that it is possible to convey them to the different organs, and then in the incorporating of these substances by these organs. We shall see later how this general concept regarding the process of nutrition, which appears to be a power of attraction in the different organ-systems for the nutritive substances, is related to the coming into existence of a single human being, the embryonic development of the single human being which takes place before birth. The most comprehensive concept of nutrition, accordingly, is this: that by means of a supersensible organism, the different nutritive substances are absorbed in the greatest variety of ways.

Now we must bear clearly in mind that man's ether-body, the supersensible member of the human organisation nearest to the physical body, is the coarsest, so to speak; but that it underlies the entire organisation as its supersensible archetype, is differentiated within itself and contains the most diverse kinds of systems of forces, in order that it may incorporate in the greatest variety of ways the substances taken in through the process of nutrition. But, in addition to this etheric organism, which we may look upon as the nearest prototype of the human organisation, we have still a higher member in the so-called astral body. (Just how these things are inter-related we shall see in the course of these lectures.) The astral body can become a member of the organism only when the physical and the etheric organisms have each been prepared according to its disposition. The astral body is that which presupposes both the other organisms. We have, moreover, the ego; so that the human being is composed of a union of these four members.

Now, we may picture to ourselves that even in the ether-body itself there are certain systems of forces that attract to themselves particles of food taken in, and then shape these in quite definite ways in the physical organism. But we can also picture to ourselves that such a system of forces is determined not only by the ether-body but also by the astral body, and that the latter sends its forces into the ether-body. If accordingly we first think away the physical organ and conceive the physical matter as cut out we have, first, the etheric system of forces and next the astral system of forces, which in turn permeates the etheric system of forces in a perfectly definite manner. Indeed we may also conceive radiations passing down into these from the ego.

Now there may be organs which are so incorporated in the whole organism that their essential characteristic, for example, lies in the fact that the etheric currents in them are, as yet, very indefinite. We find, therefore, if we investigate the space in which such an organ is located, that the etheric portion of the human organism in this spatial formation is very slightly differentiated in itself, contains very little in the way of systems of forces; but that, to make up for this, these weak forces of the ether-body are influenced by strong astral forces. When, therefore, physical matter is incorporated into such an organ as this, the ether-body exercises only a slight force of attraction and the chief forces of attraction must be exercised by the astral body upon the organ in question. It is as if the relevant substances are brought, as it were, by the astral body into this organ. From this we see that the values of the human organs here in question vary considerably. There are certain organs which we have to recognise as being determined principally through the systems of forces of the ether-body; and others which are determined, rather, through the currents or forces coming from the astral body; whereas others again are to a greater degree determined through the currents of the ego.

Now, as a result of all that has thus far been presented in these lectures one may say that especially that system of organs conveying our blood is essentially dependent upon the radiations going forth from our ego; and that the human blood, therefore, is connected essentially with the currents and radiations of the human ego. The other organ-systems, with what they contain, are determined in the greatest variety of ways by the supersensible members of man's nature.

But the reverse situation may occur when we consider the physical body *per se*, which, indeed, disregarding for the moment its higher members, exhibits likewise a system of forces. For it represents, to begin with, what we may conceive as the combination of all the substances taken in from the outer world which at the same time have brought into it their own inner forces, even though in a transformed condition. Thus the physical body is also a system of forces; so that we may also imagine cases in which this physical organism with its system of forces works back upon the etheric, or even upon the astral, system of forces, indeed even as far back as the ego-system. Not only may we conceive that the etheric system of force is seized upon by the astral- or the ego-system, but it is equally possible that there are organic systems which are specially requisitioned by the physical systems of forces, in which cases it is the physical systems of forces that prevail. Such organ-systems, in which the physical body outweighs the others, are therefore influenced to a lesser degree by the higher members of the human organisation—and more strongly influenced on the other hand by the laws of the physical body—these are more especially the organ-systems which serve in a very comprehensive sense as *organs of secretion and excretion,*[1] as glandular organs or secretory and excretory organs in general. All organs of secretion, therefore, organs which secrete substances directly in the human organism, are induced to do so—a process that has its essential significance purely in the physical world—chiefly through the forces of the physical organism. Whenever in the human body there are organs such as these, existing for the special purpose of being used by the physical organism to secrete substances, such organs, when they become diseased or are removed— which means when they become useless in some quite definite way—cause the ruin of the organism so that it cannot any longer continue its normal development.

In the case of an organ like the spleen, with regard to which the statement was ventured in yesterday's lecture that, when it becomes ill or in any way useless, its own function is

[1]*Absonderungsorgane.* The term *Absonderung* is applied in these lectures to the process whereby various organs take out a portion of the nutritive matter and hold this for use (=*secretion*) and at the same time reject the rest of the matter (=*excretion*), either discharging this portion out of the body or passing it on to be discharged. The important aspect of the process, from the point of view of these lectures, is that of separation, implying resistance, through which alone man can become conscious of himself. Hence the term *ex*cretion is used for *Absonderung* except where *se*cretion is obviously required.

affected less than would be true in the case of other organs, we see that it is very specially influenced by the supersensible portions of man's nature, by the ether-body and more especially by the astral body. And we see that in the case of some other organs the physical forces predominate. The thyroid gland, which in certain disease conditions becomes enlarged into the so-called goitre, may have a very injurious influence upon the whole organism, because the activities which it especially has to manifest are such that what it brings about in the physical world as a physical process is absolutely essential to the general economy of the human organism.

Now there may be organs that are to a very high degree dependent upon the other, the supersensible force-systems of the human organism, but which are none the less closely bound to the physical organism and are induced through its forces to secrete physical matter. Such organs, for example, are the *liver* and the *kidneys*. These are organs which, like the spleen, are dependent upon the supersensible members of the human organisation, the ether-body and the astral body, but which are seized upon by the forces of the physical organism, and are drawn downward in their activities even into the forces of the physical organism. It is, therefore, of far greater importance for them to be in a healthy condition as physical organs in the human organism than for other organs, for example, in which conditions are such that the physical demands are far outweighed by what is derived from the other members, so that we have in the spleen an organ of which we can say that it is a very spiritual organ, that is, the physical part of this organ is its least significant part. In occult literature which has come forth from circles where something was really known about these matters, the spleen has always been looked upon as a particularly spiritual organ and is described as such.

Thus we have now arrived at what we may call the concept of the "complete organ." An organ, as such, may be looked upon as a supersensible force-system; although physical-sensible substances are stored up, as it were, in the organs through the entire process of nutrition. Another concept we must acquire raises this question: What is the significance in general of taking something, whether it be a physical substance or what is received through the influence of our soul-activity; for example, through perception? And what is the significance of the excreting[1] of a physical substance?

Let us begin with the process of excretion in its most inclusive sense. We know, in the first place, that from the food taken, a large portion of the material substance is excreted. We know, further, that carbon dioxide is excreted from the human organism through the lungs; that, after the blood has been sent out of the heart and through the lungs in order to be renewed, the carbon dioxide is thrown off. We have, then, another excretory process through the kidneys, but also one through the *skin*. In this last process which goes on primarily in the forming of sweat, but also in everything occurring by way of the skin which must be classed as an excretory process, we have those excretory processes in the human being which take place at the outermost circumference of the body, its outermost periphery. Let us now ask ourselves the question: What is the full significance of the excretory process in the human being?

Only in the following way can we be clear as to the significance of a process of excretion. You will see that, without such concepts as we are developing to-day, it will be impossible for us to get any further with our study of the human organism. I should like, in order to be able gradually

1 See footnote, p. 103.

to carry forward our thinking to the essential nature of a process of excretion, first to submit for your consideration another concept which has, to be sure, only a remote similarity to the excretory processes, but which can nevertheless guide us to them, namely, the concept of the becoming aware of our Self.

Think for a moment, how is it really possible after all to affirm that there is such a thing as the becoming aware of one's Self? If you move incautiously in a room and stumble against some external object you say that you have run into something. This impact is actually a becoming aware of your own Self in such a way, that the collision has in reality become for you an inner occurrence. For what is the collision with a foreign object so far as it affects you? It is the cause of a hurt, a pain. The process of feeling pain takes place entirely within yourself. Thus an inner process is called forth by the fact that you come into contact with a foreign object, and that this constitutes a hindrance in your way. It is the becoming aware of this hindrance that calls forth the inner process which, in the moment of collision, makes itself known as pain. In fact, you can easily conceive that you do not need to know anything else whatever in order to experience this becoming aware of your Self except the effect, the pain, caused by coming into contact with an external object. Imagine that you stumble against an object in the dark without knowing at all what it is, and that you hit it so hard that you do not even stop to think what it might be, but notice only the effect in the pain. In this case you have felt the effect of the blow in such a way that you live through an inner process within yourself. You are not inwardly conscious of anything but an inner process in such a case, where you think of the blow as having taken place in the dark and of your having experienced its effect in pain.

Of course, you say to yourself "I have run into something," but this is nevertheless a more or less unconscious conclusion resulting from your inner experience which is the effect of the outer object.

From this you can see that man becomes aware of his inner Being in the *sensing of resistance*. This is the concept we must have: of becoming aware, of the consciousness of inner life, of being filled with real inner experiences through the sensing of a resistance. This is the concept which I have here developed in order to be able to make the transition to another concept, that of the excretions in the human organism. Let us suppose that the human organism takes into itself in some way or other, into one of its organ-systems, a certain kind of physical substance, and that this organ-system is so regulated that through its own activity it eliminates something from the substance taken in, separates it from the substance as a whole, so that through the activity of this organ the original complete substance falls apart into a finer, filtered portion and a coarser portion, which is excreted. Thus there begins a differentiating of the substance taken in, into a substance that is further useful, which can be received by other organs, and another that is first separated and then excreted. The unusable portions of the physical substance are thrust away in contrast with the usable portions, an expression here justified, and we have such a collision as I described roughly in the case of one's running against some outer object. The stream of physical matter as a whole, when it comes into an organ, runs against a resistance as it were; it cannot remain as it is, it must change itself. It is told by the organ, as we might say: "You cannot remain as you are; you must transform yourself." Let us suppose that such a substance goes into the liver. There it is told, "You must change yourself." A resistance is set up against it. For further use it must become a different substance, and it must cast off certain portions. Thus it happens in our organism that the substance perceives that resistance is present. Such resistances are to be found within the organism in the most diverse organs. It is only because secretion takes place at all in our organism, because we have organs of secretion, that it is possible for our organism to be secluded within itself, to be a self-experiencing being. For only so can any being become conscious of its own inner life, through the fact that its own life meets with resistance. Thus we have in the processes of secretion processes important for human life—processes, in other words, by means of which the living organism secludes itself within itself. Man would not be a Being secluded within himself if such processes of secretion did not take place.

Let us suppose that the flow of nourishment or of oxygen that has been absorbed, were to pass through the human organism as if through a tube. The result, if no resistance were offered through the organs, would be that the human organism would not be conscious within itself of its own inner life but would experience itself, on the contrary, only as belonging to the great world as a whole. We might, to be sure, imagine also that the crudest form of this resistance were to appear in the human organism, that the substance in question might knock itself against a solid wall, and turn back again into itself. This would not, however, make any difference to the inner experience of the human organism; for whether a flow of food or of oxygen were to pass through the organism, entering at one end and passing out at the other, being reflected back on itself as through a hose, this would not make any real difference to an inner experience of the human organism. That this is so we can at once gather from the fact that, when we bring it about in our nervous system that a concept turns back into itself, we thereby lift our nervous system right out of the

inner experience of the human organism. It makes no difference why the human organism is left unaffected, whether
because the streams entering from without are completely
reflected or merely pass through. What makes it possible to
realise the inner life of the human organism is the processes of
secretion.

Now if we observe that organ which we must consider the
central organ of the human organism, the organ of the blood,
noting how it continually renews the blood in one direction
by taking in oxygen, and if we see in this organ the instrument
of the human ego, we may then say that if the blood were to
go through the human ego unchanged, it could not in that case
be the instrument of the human ego, that which in the very
highest sense enables man to be conscious of his own inner
life. Only through the fact that the blood undergoes changes in
its own inner life, and then goes back as something different,
in other words, that something is excreted from the changed
blood, only because of this is it possible for man, not only
to *have an ego,* but to *experience it inwardly* with the help
of a physical-sensible instrument.

We have now enunciated the concept of the process of
excretion. We shall next have to ask ourselves how it is with
that excretion pertaining to the outermost boundary
of the human organism. It will certainly not be difficult for
us to conceive that the human organism as a whole must
operate in such a way that this excretion can take place just
where it does, on the periphery. For this purpose it is necessary that, confronting all the streams of the human organism,
there should be one organ which is connected with this most
extensive of all the processes of excretion. And this organ
which is, as you will readily surmise, the skin in its most
comprehensive sense together with everything pertaining to
it, presents most directly to the view what we call essential

in the *human form*. When we picture to ourselves, therefore, that the human organism can be inwardly conscious of its own life at its outermost periphery only through the fact that it has placed the organ of the skin where it confronts all its various streams, we are obliged to see in the peculiar formation of the skin one of the expressions of the innermost force of the human organism.

How shall we think of the skin-organ with everything pertaining to it? We shall see later in detail what it is that pertains to it, but to-day we shall characterise these relationships as a whole.

Here we must be clear about one thing. In what belongs to our conscious inner experience, about which we can still have a kind of knowledge through some sort of self-observation, there is not to be included that structure which comes to expression in the form of our skin. Even though we are still actively sharing in the fashioning of the outer surface of our body, this active sharing is such that we may say all directly voluntary action is *completely excluded.* It is true that as regards the mobility of the surface of our body, in our facial expression, gestures, etc., we have an influence which still extends to what we may call our conscious activity; but in the actual formation we no longer have any influence. It must, of course, be admitted that man does have a certain influence within narrow limits upon the outer form of his body through his inner life between birth and death. With regard to this anyone can convince himself who has known a man at a certain definite time of life, and who then sees him again after perhaps ten years. Expecially is this true if, during these ten years, this man has gone through profound inner experiences, and especially those connected with the acquiring of knowledge, not such knowledge as constitutes the subject-matter of external science, but rather those which cost blood and are connected with the destiny of the whole inner life. We then see, indeed, how within certain narrow limits the physiognomy changes; how to a certain extent, therefore, man does have within these limits an influence upon the formation of his body. Yet he has it only to a very slight degree, as anyone will have to admit; for the most essential share in the forming of man is not entrusted to his volition with the help of what reaches him through his consciousness. On the other hand we must admit that the entire human form is adapted to man's essential being. Anyone who looks into these things will never for a moment imagine that what we mean by the whole range of human capacities could develop in a being having any other form than the human form as it exists in the physical world. Everything in the way of human capacities is related to this human form. Just suppose for a moment that the frontal bone were in any other position with relation to the whole organism than what it is; in that case you would have to suppose that this different position of the frontal bone, this changing of form, would presuppose at the same time entirely different capacities and forces in man. It is possible, indeed, to make a study of this in mankind as one comes to see clearly that there are different capacities among human beings having a different outer formation of the head or other organs. This is the way, then, that we must create for ourselves a concept of the conformity of the human form to man's being in its totality, of the complete correspondence between the outer form and the essential quality of man's entire being. What lies in the forces that are active in this adaptation has nothing to do with what enters into man's own activity within the compass of his own consciousness. Since, however, man's form is connected with his spiritual activity, and with his soul-life as well, it would not be possible to imagine other-wise than that the forces which bring about the human form are those which come from another direction, to meet the forces that man himself develops within his form. Here within him are the forces of intelligence, of feeling, of temperament, etc. These the human being can develop only in the physical world, as conditioned by his particular form. This form must be given to him. Whatever capacities of ours need this form must receive it already prepared, if I may express it thus, from corresponding forces of a similar kind, which, working from the other direction, first build up the form in order that these capacities may be used as they ought to be used. It is not difficult to gain this concept. We need only think of a case like the following. When we have a machine which is to be used for some intelligent activity, some activity that has a purpose, we have to do in the first place with the machine and this purposeful activity. In order, however, that the machine may come into existence, it is necessary that similar activities be carried out, which assemble the parts of the machine and give form to the whole. These activities must be similar to those which are later carried on by means of the machine itself. We must say, therefore, that when we observe a machine it is wholly and absolutely explicable on mechanical principles; but the fact that the machine is adapted to its purpose requires us to suppose that it came into existence through the activity of a mind which had thought out that purpose beforehand. This spiritual activity has withdrawn, to be sure, and does not need to be brought forward when we wish to explain the machine scientifically; yet it is there, *behind* the machine, and first produced it.

So likewise can we say that, for the developing of our capacities and powers as human beings, we need above all those systems of forms which lie within the moulding of our organism. There must be behind this human form, however, forces that do the forming, which we can as little find in the already fashioned form as we find the builder of the machine in the machine itself.

Through this idea something else will become quite clear to you. A materialistic thinker, for instance, might come forward and say: "But why do we need to assume that there are intelligent forces and beings behind that which gives form to our physical world? We can, indeed, explain the physical world through itself, by means of its own laws: a watch or a machine, for example, can be explained by means of its own laws." Here we have arrived at a point where the worst kind of errors appear, on this side and that, where from the anthroposophical standpoint also, or among those who stand for some other spiritual world-conception, such errors occur. If it should be disputed, for example, by a spiritual-scientific world-conception that the human organism as it presents itself to us and which we are now observing according to its form, can be explained purely mechanically, or mechanistically through its own laws, that would naturally be going too far and would be quite unjustified. The human organism is, indeed, absolutely and entirely explainable out of its own laws, just as is the watch. Yet it does not follow from the fact that the watch can be explained by means of its own laws that the inventor was not behind the watch. This objection, accordingly, answers itself through the very fact that it must be admitted that the human organism must be explained on the basis of its own laws.

When we think, therefore, from the point of view of spiritual science, we have first to seek behind the form of a man as a whole for the form-creative beings—that is for what

underlies this entire human being. If we wish to form a
concept of how the human form comes to be at all, we must
think of it as coming about on the one side through the fact
that the form-giving forces unfold themselves, and that in the
building up of this human form they at first enclose themselves within it. We have presented to us, accordingly, in the
formation of the skin, the most extensive circumference
spatially of that which stands for the self-enclosing of the
formative forces in man. We might draw a sketch and think of
of these form-giving forces in man as flowing outward and enclosing themselves within the outer form, which shall here be

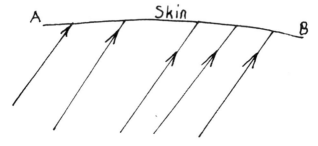

indicated simply by the line AB. It will become clear to us
that we shall have further need for this concept in order to
understand what goes on at this outermost circumference
of the human being, anywhere inside the skin. There is
something else, however, about which we must be clear: that
not only within the human skin do we find such enclosing,
but also within the human organism itself we have the same
sort of self-enclosing of the activity and fullness of being
which work into it from outside. You need only reflect
upon all that has been said up to this point and you will
remember that we do find just such self-enclosing activity
inside the human being, one in which we take no more part
than in the forming of our skin-surface. We mean here those
very activities which come about in the organs of the liver,

the gall-bladder, the spleen, etc. That which streams into the organism by means of the forces contained in the nutritive substances is stopped by these organs. Something is pushed against it; a resistance is set up in opposition to it. In other words here in these organs the external vital activity of these substances is transformed. Whereas, therefore, in the case of the form-giving forces within us, it is necessary to think of these as being active as far as the skin, and whereas outside the skin we find no more form-giving forces, we must picture to ourselves that in the case of those forces which enter into us with the stream of nutrition or air, there is not a complete enclosing of what finds its way inward as currents from without, but rather there takes place a transformation. We must not think of these organs as stopping something, as is the case with the skin, but must rather think that the vital activity of the substances is so changed by them that the stream of food taken in by these organs (*a*) is then conveyed further in a changed form (*b*) after it has met with resistance. Thus we have here to do with a process of change, and this concerns especially those particular organs which we have

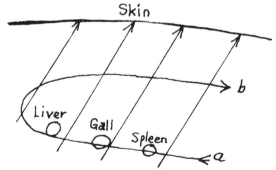

characterised as the inner cosmic system in man. They change the external movements of the substances. These are forces which, in contrast to the form-forces that build up the whole organism, we may call *forces of movement.*

Within our inner cosmic system these forces, which transform the inner vital activity of the nutritive substances, themselves become movement; so that we can rightly speak here of forces of movement in these organs.

We are now far enough advanced in our considerations to be able to say that there are forces which work from outside into the human organism, forces whose activity we cannot compass within the horizon of our consciousness. All that we can refer to as "activities" in this case takes place below the threshold of our consciousness, for certainly no one in a normal state of consciousness can observe the activity of his liver, his gall-bladder, spleen, etc. And now, since our whole nervous system is a member of our organism, the question arises: what prevents this nervous system from knowing something about the formation of the organs in this organism? This certainly does take place there; the forces that give us our form are at work in our organism, and similarly those within our inner cosmic system which change the movement and the vital activity of substances. How does it come about that we know nothing of all this?

The nervous system of our brain and spinal cord is intended, in a normal state of consciousness, to convey external impressions to the blood, that is, to take the impressions in as physical processes in such a way that these processes beat against the blood, as it were, and in doing this inscribe themselves upon the instrument of the ego, the blood, so that the outer impressions are thereby transferred to it. And just as truly the branches of the sympathetic nervous system which, with its ganglions and ramifications, stands guard over the inner cosmic system, are intended to keep the processes that go on in this inner cosmic system from approaching as far as the blood, to hold these processes back, so to speak. You have now heard something more in regard to what I have previously touched upon, namely, that the sympathetic nervous system has a function contrary to that of the nervous system of the brain and spinal cord. Whereas the latter must make the effort to convey external impressions to the blood in the best possible way, the sympathetic nervous system, with its opposite activity, must be continually holding back from the blood, from the instrument of the ego, the transformed vital activities of the substances that have been taken in. If we observe the digestive process, we have there, first, the taking in of external nutritive substances; then the holding back of the vital activities peculiar to these nutritive substances, and the transformation of these by means of the inner cosmic system of man. The vital activities of these substances, accordingly, are changed into other sorts of vital activities. In order that we need not, placed as we are in the world, continually perceive inwardly what goes on in our inner organs, this entire stream of processes must be held back from the blood by means of the sympathetic nervous system, whereas that other nervous system goes to meet what is taken in from outside.

Here, then, you have the function of the sympathetic nervous system, which becomes a part of our organism for the purpose of holding our inner processes, not allowing them to penetrate to the ego-instrument, the blood. I called your attention yesterday to the fact that the outer life and the inner life of man, as they are expressed in the ether-body, present a contrast; and that this contrast between the inner life and the outer is expressed in tensions which finally come to a climax, as we saw, in those organs of the brain called the pineal gland and the pituitary body.

Now, if you put together yesterday's and to-day's discussions, you will be able to understand that everything which beats in upon us from outside, in order to stand in the closest possible contact with the circulation of the blood, strives to unite with its counterpart, with what is held back by the sympathetic nervous system. For this reason we have, in the pineal gland, the place where what has been brought to the blood by means of the nervous system of the brain and spinal cord unites with what approaches man from the other direction; and the pituitary body is there as a last outpost to prevent the approach of what has to do with the life of the inner man. There are opposite to each other, at this point in the brain, two important organs. Everything that we live through in our inner organisation remains *below* our consciousness; for it would, indeed, be terribly disturbing to us if we were to share consciously in our whole process of nutrition. This is kept back from our consciousness by means of the sympathetic nervous system. Only when this reciprocal relationship between the two nervous systems, as this is expressed in the state of tension between the pineal gland and the pituitary body, is not in order does something result which we may call a "glimmering through from the one side to the other," a being disturbed on the one side by the other. This takes place when some irregularity in the activity of our digestive organs expresses itself in our consciousness in feelings of discomfort. In this case we have a raying into the consciousness, although very obscure, of the internal life of the human being, which has first been changed with the help of the inner cosmic system from the form it had in the life outside. Or in special emotions, such as anger and the like— which have a particularly strong influence on man, originating in the consciousness, we have a breaking through from the other direction into the organism. We then have one of these cases in which emotions, unusual inner disturbances of the soul, can influence in a specially harmful way the digestion, the respiratory system and also, consequently, the circulation of the blood and everything that lies below consciousness.

It is thus possible for these two sides of human nature to act reciprocally upon each other. And we are obliged to state that, as human beings, we actually stand in the world as a duality: a duality in the first place which has, in the nervous system of the brain and the spinal cord, instruments that bring external impressions to the blood, the instrument of the ego. From this whole stream of soul-life is held back, by means of the sympathetic nervous system, everything in the way of inner realisation of the life of the organs. These two streams confront each other all along the line, so to speak; but we find their special expressions in those two organs of which we spoke at the close of yesterday's lecture. From this point we will continue our considerations in the next lecture.

THE BLOOD AS MANIFESTATION AND
INSTRUMENT OF THE HUMAN EGO

26th March, 1911.

From the last lecture we were able to gather that man, as a physical organisation, separates himself from the outside world, to a certain extent, by means of his skin. When we conceive the human organism entirely in the light in which we have had to do during the preceding lectures, it becomes necessary to say that it is this human organism itself, with its various force-systems, which provides itself with a definite external boundary by means of the skin. In other words, we must understand clearly that the human organism is a system of forces of a nature so self-determined that it gives itself the exact outline of form which appears in the contours of our skin. We shall have to say, therefore, that in connection with the life-process of man there is the interesting fact that in the outer border of the form we have, expressed in a picture, as it were, the combined activity of all the force-systems of the organism. If, on the other hand, the skin itself is to be such an expression of the organism, then we should have to presuppose that it must actually be possible in some way to find the whole man, in a certain sense, in the skin. For, if man as he exists is so to construct himself that the outer skin, as the boundary of his form, expresses what he is, it must in that case be possible to find in the skin everything belonging to his total organisation. As a matter of fact, if we look into what belongs to this total organisation of man, we shall find out how true it is that everything is present in the skin, inside the skin itself, which is present as a tendency in the force-systems of the entire organism.

In all the preceding we have seen that the whole man, in his appearance as earth-man, has in his blood-system the instrument of the ego, so that he actually is *man* by reason of the fact that he harbours within himself an *ego,* and that this ego can create an expression of itself as far as the physical system, can work with the blood as its instrument. And now, if the surface of the body, the boundary of the form, is an essential member of the whole organisation, we must conclude that this whole organisation must be active by means of the blood as far as the skin, in order that an expression of the whole human being in so far as he is physical can exist. If we observe the skin—and we must understand it as consisting of several layers stretched over the entire surface of the body—we find that, as a matter of fact, fine blood vessels do extend into this skin, and we are therefore obliged to conclude that it is by means of these fine blood vessels which extend into the skin that the ego is able to send out its forces and create for itself, through the blood, an expression of the human being extending as far as the skin. We know, furthermore, that the nervous system is the physical instrument for everything which we may characterise as consciousness. And, inasmuch as the boundary of the bodily surface is an expression of the plan of the human being as a whole, the nerves must also reach out into the skin-boundary in order that man may express himself adequately in this skin-boundary. We see, therefore, spreading out close to the fine blood vessels lying within the layers of the skin, the nerve-terminations, commonly although not quite correctly called tactile corpuscles, because it is believed that with the help of these man perceives the external world through the sense of touch, just as he perceives light and sound through the eye and the ear. Such is not the case, however, and we shall see later what the facts really are.

Thus we find present in the skin what constitutes the expression, or the bodily organ, of the human ego; and we find also what constitutes the expression of human consciousness reaching out into the skin in the form of fine nerves and their projections. Then we must look around for the expression of what we may consider as the instrument of the life-process. We have already in our last lecture directed attention to this instrument of the life-process, in our discussion of the function of secretion. In this function, in which we have seen that a sort of hindering takes place, as it were, we may recognise the expression of the life-process, to the extent that a living being which wills to exist in the world is compelled to shut itself off from the outside world. This self-enclosing can take place only by its experiencing a hindering within itself. This living through a hindrance in itself is brought about by means of the organs of secretion, which may be described in the broadest sense as *glands*. Glands are organs of secretion; and, in so far as they are such, there takes place in them that sort of hindrance which calls forth inner resistance, in order that a being may shut itself off within itself. We must presuppose, therefore, that such organs of secretion, similar to those we have everywhere else in the organism, belong also to the skin. And they do belong to the skin; for we find, in the skin organs of secretion, glands of the greatest possible variety, which carry on this function of secretion, in other words, a life-process, within the skin.

Now, if we ask finally what underlies this life-process, we shall find there something we may call a purely material process, that is, the conveying of substances from one organ to another. At this point we must differentiate carefully between a process such as has to do with *life* and is a process of secretion, which creates an inner hindrance, and that process which transports substances quite externally, which causes a transference of substances from one organ to another. These are not the same. To a materialistic conception it might seem as if they were, but to a living grasp of reality they are not so. As long as we are alive we are not dealing, in a single member of the human organisation, with a mere transportation of substances from one organ to another. In the very moment, when the nutritional substances are absorbed by the life-process, we are dealing with the most intimate events which occur. Thus we come down a step from the real life-process to the process of the physical body when we say that this process of secretion, looked at *physically,* is such that the substances of nutrition which are taken in are transported to all the different parts of the physical body; whereas in its other aspect it is a living activity, a becoming aware of itself, as it were, on the part of the organism in its own inner being, through the setting up of hindrances. Through the life-processes there takes place at the same time a transporting of substances, and we find this in the skin just as in the other parts of the organism. The nutritive substances are continually being secreted, carried outwards in the skin, and there also excreted through the process of perspiration, so that here also what we may call a transporting in the physical sense, a changing of the substances in the organism, is physically present.

We have thus set forth in its essence the fact that even in the external organ of the skin are present both the blood-system, as the expression of the ego, and the nervous system as the expression of the consciousness. And now I wish little by little to direct you to the fact that we have a right to bring together all phenomena of consciousness under the expression "astral body," that is, to conceive the nervous system comprehensively as an expression of the astral body; that we have what we may call the glandular system as an expression of the ether-body, or life-body; and the actual process of nutrition and depositing of substances as an expression of the physical body. To this extent all the separate members of the human organism are actually present in the skin-system, through which man shuts himself off from the outside world. Now, we must take into account the fact that all such divisions of the human organisation as the blood-system, the nervous system, the nutritive system, etc., form a *whole*; through their interrelationships and that when we observe these four systems of the human organisation and have them before us in the physical body, we are viewing the human organism in two aspects, as it were. We actually have it before us in two aspects and in such a way, indeed, that we may say that the human organism has meaning within our earth-existence only if, as an entire organism, it is the instrument of the ego. It can be this, however, only if the most immediate instrument which the human ego can employ, the blood-system, is present in it.

We can state thus that the blood-system is the most immediate instrument of the human ego. Yet the blood-system is possible only if all the other systems are first existent. The blood is not only, according to the meaning of the poet's words, "a very special fluid"; it is also obvious that it cannot exist as it is except by finding a place for itself in the entire remaining organism; its existence must necessarily be prepared for by all the rest of the human organism. The blood, as it exists in man, cannot be found anywhere else than in the human organism. We shall refer, further on, to the relation of the human blood to the blood of the animal; and this will be a very important consideration, since external science to-day takes little notice of it. To-day we are dealing with blood as the expression of the human ego, taking account, at the same time, of a remark which was made in the first lecture: namely, that what is here said concerning man cannot, without further thought, be applied to any other kind of earth-being whatever. We may say then that, when once the entire remaining organism of man is constructed as it is, it is then capable of receiving into itself the circulatory course of the blood, is capable, that is, of carrying the blood, of having within itself that instrument which is the tool of our ego. The whole human organism, however, must first be built up for this purpose.

As you know, there are other beings on the earth which seem to have a certain kinship with man, but which are not in a position to bring to expression a human ego. In their case it is obvious that what appears similar in these other systems to human potentialities is built up otherwise than in the human being. To put it somewhat differently: in all of these systems which precede the blood-system there must first be present everything, in a preparatory plan, which is capable of receiving the blood. This means that we must have a nervous system exactly fitted to receive a blood-system such as that of *man*; we must have a glandular system which is perfectly prepared for the circulation of human blood; and the system of nutrition must likewise be thoroughly prepared for the human blood-system. This signifies in turn, however, that even from the other aspect of man's organism, for example, the whole nutritional system, which we have described as expressing the actual physical body of man, there must be present the potentiality of the ego. The entire process of nutrition must, as it were, be so directed and guided through the organism that the blood can finally move

in the courses which are right for it.
What does that mean?

Let us assume, since everything is absolutely determined in its formation
and its particular kind of activity by the
quality of man's being, that we had to
draw the course of the blood (in a mere
diagram, of course) in this fashion. We
should then have to say that this circulation of the blood must now be received by the rest of the organism,
which must fit itself into this. This
means that all the other systems of organs must be directed to the very place,
or to the neighbourhood, where the
blood has to be. We could not have the
whole texture of the blood-vessels, as
this exists in our head for example, or
in some other part of our organism,

if what is necessary to it were not in each case directed just
where the blood is to circulate. That is, the force-systems
(which I here indicate by a second line) must act in the
human organism, beginning with the nutritive system, in
such a way that they carry all the nutritive matter to the
proper places, and at the same time so form it beforehand
that in these places, by means of such preparation of the
nutritive matter, the blood-system can hold exactly to the
form of the course it now takes, and thereby be an expression
of the ego. There must, accordingly, be contained in all the
impulses of our nutritive apparatus, that is, our lowest
organ-system, just that thing which makes of man an *ego*. In
other words, the entire form which man finally presents to
us must be incorporated in what we call the various methods

of nutrition. Here we are looking down from the blood into the organ-systems which prepare the circulatory course of the blood, far, far down, from our ego to those processes which go on in the darkness of our organism. Although our blood is the expression of our ego-activity, the most conscious activity in us, it is at the same time necessary to look down into the obscure depths of our organism and say that the way in which our organism down there is built up and formed through other processes, concerning which we do not know at all how the different substances are carried to those places where they ought to be, in order that our organism may be constructed by the several force-systems just as the ego desires to have it—this shows us that, beginning with the nutritive processes, there are present in man's organism all the laws which lead ultimately to the formation of the course of the blood.

Now, the blood presents to us the most mobile, the most active, of all our systems. We know, indeed, that even if we interfere only very slightly with the course of the blood, it follows at once another direction from the one it takes in the normal course. We need only prick ourselves and the blood at once takes another direction from its usual one. This is of infinite importance; for we can see from it that the blood is the most easily controlled element in the human body; that it has a good foundation in the other organic systems while at the same time it is the most controllable of the all, has the least stability within itself, and is more determined than any other system by the experiences of the conscious ego. I shall not now go into the fantastic theories of external science concerning blushing or turning pale from feelings of shame or anxiety; I shall merely point to the purely external fact that, underlying such experiences as fear or anxiety, or the feeling of shame, are ego-experiences which are recognisable in their effect upon the blood. With the feeling of fear or anxiety it is as if we wanted to guard ourselves, so to speak, against something which we believe will have an influence upon us: we draw back with our ego. With the feeling of shame we would best of all like to hide ourselves, to obliterate our ego. In both cases, referring only to the external facts, the blood, as an external physical instrument, follows physically what the ego lives through in itself. In the case of feelings of fear and anxiety, where a man would like to draw back into himself completely, from something which he feels to be threatening him, he becomes pale; the blood draws back to its centre, draws inward. When a man would like to hide himself because of his sense of shame, would like to obliterate his ego, or best of all not to exist, or to slink away somewhere, the blood, under the influence of what the ego may here live through, spreads out as far as the periphery. And so you see from this that the blood is the most easily controllable system in man, and that it can follow in a definite way the experiences of the ego.

Now, the deeper we penetrate into the organ systems, the less do these systems follow our ego in this way, the less are they inclined to adapt themselves wholly to the inner experiences of the ego. Whatever especially affects the nervous system is regulated as we know along certain definite nerve-courses, and these nerve-courses show us something relatively fixed, in their functioning, in contrast to the blood. Whereas the blood is mobile, and can be guided under the influence of ego-experiences from one part of the body to another, as happens in the case of shame and fear, we must say, with regard to the nerve-courses, that the forces which are active here must be the forces of consciousness, and that these forces cannot carry the nerve-substance from one place to another as can be done with the blood-substance. This substance of the nervous system is, indeed, more fixed than the substance of the blood.

And this is still more true in the case of the glandular system, which shows us glands that have certain definite tasks to perform in definite places within the organism. If a gland has to be brought into activity by some means or other to some definite purpose, it cannot be aroused by means of some such cord as the nerve-cord; rather it must be stimulated at the very place where it is situated. That which is contained in the glandular system, therefore, is even more fixed than the nerves; we must excite the glands where they are. Whereas we can guide the activity of the nerves along the nerve-cords (we have in this system connecting fibres also, which unite the separate ganglions), the gland must be looked for where it is located.

Still more striking, however, is this process of fixation, this process of being inwardly determined (not "being determinable") in everything that has to do with the system of nutrition, by means of which man incorporates substances directly into himself in order to be a physical, sensuous being. For this incorporating of substances there must, nevertheless, be available a thorough preparation for the instrument of the ego as well as for the other instruments.

Thus, when we observe the human organism primarily with reference to its lowest system, the nutritive system, in its broadest sense, by means of which the substances within the organism are conveyed to all its various members, we may say that these substances must be so distributed that the formation, the external structure, of the man may proceed in a manner which finally renders possible the manifestation of the ego within this human organisation. To this end much is necessary. It is necessary not only that the substances of nutrition be conveyed in the most diverse ways, that they be deposited in all the different parts of the organism; but also that all possible provision be made to determine the outer form of the human organism.

Now, it is important that we should be clear as regards the following: in what we have called the skin are represented indeed, as we have found, all the systems of the human organism, so that we have been able to come even to the lowest system itself, the nutritive system, and to say that everything which in the strictest sense belongs to the physical system of man, considered as the system of nutrition, is poured into the skin. Yet you can easily understand that this skin as such, in spite of the fact that it has all these other systems in it, has one great defect. It does, to be sure, correspond to the form of the human organism; yet, of itself alone, it would not have this form. In spite of the fact that it has all the organ-systems in itself, it would not of itself be capable of giving to man the outline of his form. If that alone were present which is present in the skin, man would collapse, through it alone he could not maintain his upright form. From this we see that not only are there necessary those nutritive processes which make the skin a physical system, but that other manifold nutritive processes must also be possible which determine the form of the human organism as a whole. At this point, therefore, it will not be difficult to grasp the fact that we must consider those nutritive processes which go on in the *cartilage* and the *bones* as such transformed nutritive processes. What sort of processes are they?

When the matter contained in our nutritive substances is conducted to a cartilage or a bone, it is really transported only as physical matter; and what we ultimately find in the cartilage or the bone is nothing else than the transformed nutritive substances. Here, however, they are transformed differently than in the skin. We must, therefore, conclude that we have, in the skin, transformed nutritive substances which are deposited in the outermost boundary of our body, following the outline of its form, for the purpose of making us into physical man; yet, on the other hand, through the way in which the nutritive matter is deposited in the bones, we must also see that there we have to do with a nutritive process which rounds out the human form but which, in comparison with that expressed in the skin, is a different transformation of the nutritive process. And now, if we follow the method of observation we used earlier in connection with the nervous system, we will have no difficulty in understanding this entire nutritive process and the trans-portation system for the nutritional substances.

When we look at the skin, which finally shuts man off from the outside world, and when we observe the nutri-tive substances that bring about that external enclosure which in itself certainly provides man with his surface structure, but which could not of itself produce the human form, it then becomes clear that this nutritive process which is active in the skin is the most recent one in the human organism. In the manner of providing nourishment to the bones we see a process which bears a relationship to the process of nourish-ment in the skin similar to that which we attributed to the process of the formation of the brain as compared with the formation of the spinal cord. Just as the brain appeared to us to be the older organ, and the spinal cord the younger, and the brain appeared to be a metamorphosed spinal cord, so here we have a right to say: if that same thing which we see as the latest, external process of skin-formation is imagined metamorphosed at a maturer stage we can then recognise this in the firmer, self-solidifying process of nourishment which appears in the building up of the cartilage and the shaping of the bones.

This observation of the human organism might, therefore, point us to the following conception, namely, that what to-day appears before us as the bony system, in which the process of nourishment shows us a quality of inner stability, an earthy quality, so to speak, this bony system actually did, at an earlier stage, also develop in a softer substance; and only later did it become hard and take on the form of the firm bony system. This can be indicated even by external science, which teaches us that certain forms which in later life are quite clearly bones in the human organism are in the early years of childhood still soft, have the quality of cartilage. This means, therefore, that out of a softer, cartilaginous mass the bones are formed, as a result of the deposition of a different sort of nutritive matter from that which is deposited in the mass of cartilage. Here we have, indeed, a transition from a softer to a firmer form, as this process still goes on to-day in the individual human life. If we see, then, in the cartilage an earlier stage of the bone, we may say that the whole deposition of the bony system in the organism appears to us as something representing a last result, as it were, of those processes appearing in the nourishing of the skin. First, the substances must in the simplest way be metamorphosed to the softest possible substance and driven toward the organs of the body; and, when this preparation has taken place, the nutritive process then can go on, and certain parts can be hardened into bony matter, in order that the form of the human organism as a whole may be the final result.

The nature of the bones as we see them, on the other hand, gives us the right to conclude from direct evidence that really we can find no further progress in the nutritive process beyond that in the bony formation, in so far as the human being, up to the present stage of his evolution, is concerned. Whereas we have in the content of the blood the most determinable substance in man, we have in the bony substance, in that which appears before us in the form of the bones, something which is not determinable, which has arrived at a stage of maximum fixity of form. Indeed, if we continue our previous observations, that the blood is man's most easily controlled instrument whereas the nerves are less subject to his influence, we must then consider that in the bony system, which is the foundation of the entire human organization, we have something that has arrived at the ultimate stage in its evolution so far as man of to-day is concerned, something which represents the product of a final metamorphosis. For this reason, moreover, everything which has to do with forming the bony system, in spite of the fact that this must be wholly directed toward the ego, must take place in such a way that the bones may be ultimately the carriers and supporters of an organism like this, in order that the courses of the blood may take such directions as they should, and this in turn in order that in these courses of the blood the human ego may have a proper instrument.

I should like to ask who would not look upon the human organism with the greatest admiration, and say: "I have here before me that which must have gone through the greatest number of transformations, the greatest number of stages, which must have begun with the lowest stage of a process of nutrition and finally have ascended, through countless epochs, as far as the bony system, which at length has been so constructed that it can be the firm bearer, the firm supporter of the ego!" Once we become aware of how the tendency of the ego works even in the forming of the separate bones, so that man can ultimately become an *ego-bearer,* who of us would not be filled with admiration before this edifice of the human organism and say: "When we observe this human being we find we have two poles, as it were, of physical existence represented in the blood-system, which is the most subject to outside influence, and the bony system, which is in itself the most solid of all, the one which has gone farthest in the state of impermeability to influence." In this bony system of man the physical organisation has found the final expression of itself, an ultimate conclusion, whereas in the blood-system the human physical organisation has, in a certain sense and at its present stage of existence, made a new beginning.

When we look at our bony system, we can truly say that we revere it as an ultimate conclusion of the human physical organisation. And, when we look at our blood-system, we can say that we see in it a beginning, something which could begin only after all the other systems of the organisation were there first. We may say with regard to the bony system: "Its first beginning must already have been present, as a soft substance, before the glands could be given a place; for the glands had, indeed, to be supported at their appropriate places by the bone-forces; and such was the case likewise with the courses of the nerves and the blood. The bony system is the oldest of the force-systems belonging to the human organism; consequently it is the foundation of our organisation."

If, therefore, we observe these two extremes in the human organisation, we find we have in the blood-system the most mobile element, the element which is so active within us that to a certain extent it follows every inner stirring of the ego; and in the bony system we have something almost entirely withdrawn from that over which our ego still has any influence, we can no longer reach it with our ego; yet in spite of this, the whole organisation of the ego is contained within its form. Hence, even to purely external observation, the blood-system and the bony system in man are like a beginning and a conclusion in contrast to each other. And, if we thus look at ourselves, having a blood-system which continually obeys all the stirrings of the ego, we must conclude that human life really expresses itself in this active blood. And when we look at our bony system we say: "It really is somewhat isolated; it is that which draws aloof from our human life, and serves it only as a support." Or, to express it differently: "Our pulsating blood is our life; our bony system is that which has already withdrawn from a direct connection with our life, because of its ancient origin; has already eliminated itself, and continues merely to serve as a support, to give us form." Whereas in our blood we are *alive,* we are in truth already *dead* in our bony system. And I urge you to look upon this expression as a *leitmotiv* for the lectures which follow, for it will help us to certain important physiological conclusions: "Whereas in our blood we are alive, we are in our bony system, strictly speaking, already dead!" Our bony system is like a scaffolding, the thing in us that is least of all alive, only a scaffolding to support us.

We have seen in man from the first a *duality.* And here this duality confronts us in yet another form: we have, on the one hand, in our blood that which is the most vitally active, the most living thing in man; and, on the other, we have in our bony system something which draws aloof from this vital activity of ours, something which really already bears death in itself. Moreover it is, in a certain sense, our bony system which is least subordinated in its form to the life of the ego. For this reason the bony system has already arrived, in its form, at a certain final conclusion, even though it still continues to grow, at that stage in a human life when the ego-experiences first begin to stir inwardly. By the time of the change of teeth the bony system has taken its form in the main; it then merely continues to develop by growth those forms which it has produced. In the forming of the new teeth, somewhere about the seventh year, we have the last productive activity of which the bony system is capable. During that very time when we ourselves still remain withdrawn from our inner vital activity, the chief development of our bony system is proceeding.

It is then, moreover, that most mistakes are made in the giving of nutrition, when the bony system is building itself out of the dark foundations and forces of the organism. The way is prepared in these years for bone-diseases such as rickets and the like, if the processes of nourishment are not properly directed. Thus we see that what is withheld from the ego works into our bony system.

It is entirely different in the case of the blood-system, which follows in active response the life of the individual human being and is more dependent than any other system upon the processes of our conscious inner life. It is a fallacy on the part of external science to believe that the nervous system is more susceptible to inner experiences than is the blood-system. I shall here point only to the fact that in a phenomenon such as blushing, where a shifting of the blood takes place, we have the very simplest form of the influencing of the blood-system by way of the ego-experiences; likewise, when we become pale from anxiety and fear, we have transitory expressions of ego-experiences clearly manifested in the instrument of the ego. The way the ego feels in fear or shame is expressed through its instrument, the blood. You can understand, therefore, if such expressions occur even in the merely transitory processes, that the more lasting, habitual experiences of the ego must certainly manifest themselves in the easily excitable element of the blood. There is no passion, no instinct, no emotion, whether we experience these habitually or whether they come to expression in an explosive way, which does not pass over, as inner experience, to the blood as the instrument of the ego, which does not there express itself externally. All the unwholesome elements of the inner life of the ego express themselves primarily in the blood-system. And so, wherever we wish to understand anything that goes on in the blood-system, it is important not merely to inquire as to the nutritive process but even more to look into the soul-processes in so far as they are inner ego-experiences, such as moods, habitual passions, emotions and the like. Only the materialist will direct his attention chiefly to the nutrition in connection with disturbances in the blood-system. For the nourishment of the blood is dependent upon that of the physical system, the glandular system, the nervous system, and the rest; and, as a matter of fact, the nutritive matter is already thoroughly filtered when it comes into the blood. If therefore the blood is to be adversely affected from without, the organism must already be in a seriously diseased state. On the other hand all soul-processes, all processes of the ego, react directly upon what is occurring in the circulation of the blood.

Thus our bony system is the one which most of all draws aloof from the processes of our ego, while our blood-system accommodates itself more than any other to these ego-processes. Indeed this bony system is by nature, we might say, quite independent of the human ego, and yet adapted to its purpose, with the exception of one single portion which, just because it presents an exception to the characteristic of the bony system of not being determinable by the ego, has given cause for all sorts of mischief.

You know that there is such a thing as "Phrenology," an investigation of the skull. This bone-investigation, in spite of the fact that, from a certain materialistic point of view, it is looked upon as superstition, has gradually, even where loyally fostered, taken on a materialistic colouring in accordance with the general fashion of our time. If we were disposed to characterise it somewhat crudely we might say: Phrenology is carried on in general in such a way that the expression of the inner nature of the ego is sought for in the forms in which the skull is moulded. Thereby certain general principles are set up, that one prominence in the skull signifies this, another that, and so forth. The human qualities are sought for in the light of these prominences, so that phrenology seeks in the bony system of the skull for a kind of plastic expression of the ego. And yet, if it is carried on in this way, even though it seems to look for spiritual expressions in the structure of the single bones, it is harmful. For anyone who is a truly keen observer knows that *no* single human skull is like another, and that no one could ever account for this or that by way of generic elevations or depressions. Every separate skull is so different from every other that in each we find different forms.

Now, we have stated that whereas the blood in its vital activity is the system that most of all follows the ego, the bony structure withdraws from it, follows it least of any. Any yet, although the bones in general appear to be designed according to type, the skull-bones and also the bones of the face seem in a certain way to correspond to the human ego. Anyone who observes the structure of the skull knows, at the same time, that although man himself is an individual and his skull-structure is also individual, yet this wonderful configuration of the skull has been designed from the beginning in accordance with the particular human individuality and must develop just as the other bones do—only in a different form for each man. How does this come about? It comes about for the same reason that underlies the development of the individual qualities of man in general; for the entire life of the individual human being does not run its course only from a birth to a death, but continues throughout many incarnations. Whereas our ego has no influence, therefore, over the skull-structure in our present incarnation, it has developed during the intervening period between the last death and the last birth in accordance with the experiences of the preceding incarnation, the forces which determine the skull-structure; and it is these forces which determine the form of the skull in *this* incarnation. What the ego was in the preceding incarnation determines the form of the skull in *this* one; so that in the structure of our skull we have an external plastic expression of the way in which we, every single one of us, again however as individuals, have lived and acted in the preceding incarnation. Whereas all the other bones we have in us express something which is common to man, the skull in its external form expresses that which we were in an earlier incarnation.

Thus the element of the blood, which is the most vitally active of all, can be determined by the ego in *this* incarnation; our bones, on the other hand, have already entirely withdrawn during this incarnation from the influence of the ego, with the exception of the last remaining case of the skull-bone which also, however, no longer follows the ego in this incarnation, except only as the ego carries over its own evolution from the one incarnation into the next, and so develops the formative forces in the interval between the two that it can manifest in these very bones what was our nature and character in the preceding incarnation. There is no such thing as a general phrenology; but, to sum up, we must judge every man according to what he himself is; and the structure of our skull we must look upon as a work of art. Of course we are compelled to recognise something individual in the skull-structure; yet at the same time an individual something that is an expression of the ego of a preceding incarnation.

Thus we see that even this form of bone-structure, as it appears in the structure of the skull, is withdrawn from the blood to such an extent that the ego has no more influence over it excepting only during the passing between death and a new birth, when the ego receives, after death, still stronger forces with which to overcome and shape for itself those forces that have already completely withdrawn from the vital activity in the man. When, therefore, anyone speaks about the idea of reincarnation and says: "That is something which, speaking generally, is beyond our judgment or reason," one may answer: "You can, if you will, convince yourself by tangible evidence that the human ego was present in a previous incarnation. When you take hold of a human head you have before you the tangible proof of reincarnation!" And anyone who does not admit this, who sees something paradoxical in the fact that, because of the way in which a thing is formed externally, the way a thing appears in its outward form, one is forced to infer something living that formed this exterior shape out of its own inner life, such a person has no right to deduce in any other case a living something when he comes across a modelled form. He who cannot admit as strictly logical the conclusion that in the form of our individual skull is expressed the configuration of our ego of preceding incarnations has also no right, if he finds a shell, for example, to conclude from its form that at one time there was a living being in it! And anyone who does so conclude dare not dismiss the logical and absolutely equivalent conclusion that, in the individual plastic formation of a man's cranium, direct proof is given of the influence of an earlier life on the present one.

Thus you see that we have here one of the means by which to throw light by means of physiology upon the idea of reincarnation. We must only give ourselves time. If we are patient and wait, we shall discover where proofs may be procured, and how to procure them. And anyone who might be disposed to deny that there is logic in what has just been stated would have to disown all palaeontology; for it rests on the same inference. Thus we see how, by penetration into the forms of the human organisation, we can trace it back to its spiritual foundations.

THE CONSCIOUS LIFE OF MAN

27th March, 1911.

We have been able, in the course of these lectures, to form the impression that the different systems of organs and structural parts of the human being participate in the greatest variety of ways in the combination of processes within the organism. We have referred to various facts in this connection, and have found ourselves already compelled to ascribe as a preliminary the activities at work in the different systems of organs to higher, supersensible members of the human organism. We had to assert, for instance, that in man the circulation of the blood bears an intimate relation to what we call the human ego, so that we had to speak of the blood as an instrument of the human ego; and, further, we have been able to attribute to the nervous system everything which as conscious life comes to meet this ego. We have at the same time shown how one special portion of the nerve-system, the sympathetic nerve-system, has a function to a certain extent contrary to that of the rest of this system, a function which consists in holding back everything that goes on in the depths of man's organisation, everything that is brought about by the activity of the members of the inner cosmic system in man, so that for the normal consciousness it does not at first force its way up to the horizon of the ego. Yesterday, moreover, we attempted to arrive at an approximate understanding of the fact that what has constructed itself into the firm bony scaffolding, withdraws itself most of all from this conscious life of man; yet at the same time we had to emphasise the fact that, even in this solid scaffolding, a quality of Being must be active such as enables man to evolve an organ for the life of his ego, namely, the circulation of the blood.

We may, therefore, draw the conclusion that the significance of the depositing of the bony system in man, as related to his whole organisation, consists in the fact that he can maintain a human form at all; and that everything expressed in the processes which take place in this solid bony system is kept in the subconscious. We have always to do with something of this kind in the human organisation, and we must be especially clear that something within it is shielded from the influences that play a part in our environment in the great world. We have stated, for example, that the seven members of the inner cosmic system, especially that most spiritual one among them, the spleen, restrain the working of the external laws natural to what we take in as nourishment; that they convey the nutritive substances into the organism in such a manner that they are finally filtered into a form which enables them to exert their powers in conformity with laws and a vital activity of their own. This shielding of the inner processes, this transforming and implanting of outside matter, is most visible and obvious in the warmth of the blood. This blood-warmth, which operates within strict limits of temperature, is regulated by conformity to its own inner laws; and, in this conformity it is, in normal life, independent of what takes place in the warmth-processes of the macrocosm, of the great world about us. Here in the stability of the temperature of the blood we have a perfectly obvious fundamental phenomenon. We must point out, therefore, that one of the most essential elements in the inner organisation of man is that something possessed of Being is cut off within set limits from the macrocosm and develops a vital activity of its own.

Now in order to advance still further in our understanding of the human organism, it will be well for us to-day to proceed for a short while from another direction, so as to direct our attention briefly to the *conscious* life. We know already from the preceding lectures that the conscious life of man employs the instruments of the blood and the nervous system. We have not, however, been able to go into the finer processes; for this investigation is something, we must frankly confess, still liable to startle the outside world which so depends upon present-day customary science. On the other hand, anyone who has a basis of genuine and true occultism will tell you that the tendency of modern science is leading toward a confirmation, in the course of the next few decades, of those things which we are able to bring forward at the present time, though, to be sure, only through occult observations. If I could hold lectures for half a year, instead of this short series, it would be possible out of the findings of modern science alone to bring forward all that is necessary for external proof of what must be only briefly intimated to-day.[1] As it is, however, I must leave very much to the good will of my audience. It is possible, indeed, in the case of everything stated here, to trace our way to external science which is already in a position, provided it begins with facts and not theoretical prejudices, to discover confirmation, on the basis of its present-day findings, for what may be learned in the sphere of occultism.

Now if we are to start out from our conscious life—and I beg you to understand all these discussions as having such a basis and to consider the relation of the more or less

1 See *Grundlegendes für eine Erweiterung der Heilkunst nach geisteswissenschaftlichen Erkentnissen*, 1925 Philosophisch-Anthroposophischer Verlag, Dornach.

conscious soul-life to our organism—we must keep in mind, as indeed is done in ordinary physiology, all that we call our *thought-activity* in its most comprehensive sense. We do not need in this connection to go into all the niceties of logical and psychological distinctions, but must simply realise that we have here to do with the thought-life of man, and furthermore, within the realm of our soul's life, with the life of feeling and willing.

You will never find any contradiction among those who have a foundation of true occultism, when it is asserted that all processes in our soul-life which take place on the physical plane, and which fall into any one of the categories of our thinking, feeling, or willing life, are accompanied, in a normal state of consciousness, by actual *material* processes in the organism, whether endued with life or not. We may find, therefore, that for literally everything which takes place in our soul there are corresponding material processes within our organism. And it is precisely this fact that is of the very greatest interest. For it will be for the first time possible in the next few decades, as a result of certain tendencies in contemporary science, for the present still only tendencies, actually to discover these correspondences between soul-processes and physiological processes, and thus to confirm what we have attained through occultism.

For every thought-process there is a corresponding process within our organism; and the same is true in the case of every emotional process, and every process which may be denoted as an "impulse of will." We might put it in this way: whenever something takes place in our soul-life it produces a wave which repeats itself as far down as the physical organism. Let us take first the process of thinking, what occurs in thought. And here I wish to call attention to the fact that it is best to fix our minds upon a thought process that is either purely mathematical, or one which is equally objective and which leaves our feeling and willing in a certain sense uninfluenced; that is, we shall first consider thought-processes in pure and unalloyed form. What happens in our organism when such thought-processes go on within our soul-life? Every time we fix upon a thought, there takes place in our organism a process which we may compare with another one of a different kind; by this I do not mean that what I am here stating is an analogy, for it is not an analogy, but an actual fact; and, when I say "we may compare" I mean that this comparison is to lead us to the facts of the matter. We may compare it with what takes place when we dissolve any kind of salt in a glass of water heated to a certain temperature, and by allowing this water to cool cause the salt to crystallise, thus bringing about the very opposite of the process of solution. When the salt is entirely dissolved the water is transparent; but when the water has cooled again, and the opposite process takes place in it, the salt separates itself from the water and crystallises again. There comes about a re-formation of the salt, a depositing of salt in the water. And when we observe water which at first was warm and then is brought to a state in which the salt recrystallises in it, we see that there within the liquid a solid substance takes form. Something solid settles again, a salt-deposit. (As I said before, I have taken it for granted that these statements as to results of occult research will at first startle anyone who accepts quite pedantically, and in a purely conventional way, the facts recorded by external science.)

Now exactly the same process takes place within our organism when we *think*. This corresponding process of thinking is a salt-depositing process, so to speak, which is caused by a certain activity in our blood and which irritates and reacts upon our nerve-system, a process, that is, which goes on on the "frontiers" between our blood- and nerve-systems. And just as we can look at the water in the glass and observe the formation of the salt as it separates and crystallises, so we may see, when we observe a human being exercising thought, that just such a process, supersensibly perceptible in all its exactness to the clairvoyant eye, actually does take place. Thus we have here brought before our minds the physical correlative of the process of thought.

At this point we may ask what is the nature of the corresponding correlative of *feeling*? Here we do not have to do with a depositing of solidifying salt, which is the opposite of the process of solution; but we find that within our organism what we may call refined processes take place which are somewhat like that of a fluid becoming *semi-solid*. Let us imagine, for instance, a fluid which is just solid enough to take on form—about as much form as there is in very thick albumen: a coagulation, that is, or the thickening of a fluid. Whereas, in the case of thought-processes, we have to do with the direct production of a salt-substance which is deposited out of a fluid, in everything pertaining to feeling we have to do with a transition from an inwardly more fluid state to a semi-fluid one. The substance is here transformed into a somewhat more dense condition which, with clairvoyant sight, may be identified as the formation of small flakes, just as if, in a glass containing a fluid, you were to bring about through certain processes the process of a flake-formation, or an inner changing of a fluid substance into tiny semi-liquid drops.

When we go on to what we may call the cherishing of a will-impulse in the soul, we find that the physical correlative of this again is different. It is, moreover, even easier to grasp; in fact, we come here to that aspect in which the physical is considerably more manifest. The physical correlative of what conforms to will-impulse is a sort of warming-process, a process, indeed, which in some way or other produces certain degrees of heightened temperature within the organism, a becoming hot, in a certain sense. Now we may also conclude from this, since this becoming warm is connected with the whole pulsation of our blood, that it is precisely and altogether with this that the impulses of the will are connected. It is not very difficult, if one has even only a moderate capacity for true observation, to be able actually to see that such processes, both in the human and also in the animal organisation, can have their physical correlatives.

Thus we may to a certain extent characterise in this way the physical correlatives which accompany the inner soul-process. What I have just been characterising is obviously not something of a crude physical nature, but rather extraordinarily fine and minute processes, fine to such a degree, indeed, as cannot usually be imagined. With the exception, perhaps, of the processes of warmth, they are of such a nature that, in comparison with all that we know of similar processes in the outside physical world, they manifest an extreme delicacy. They are processes which the organism carries out by means of all its forces, when the ego is active, with the help of the instrument of the blood: from the process of salt-depositing to the coagulation of fluid and the producing of warmth. They are in part of such a nature that we might say the entire organism is affected by them; or, in the case of the thinking process for example that one part of our organisation, the brain or the spinal cord, is chiefly affected by them. Moreover these processes, which are the results of the influence of soul-processes, are distributed in the most varied way possible in the human organism. When

we gradually learn to know that these are facts we come to
the point where we are compelled to admit that what we call
thoughts or feelings are actual forces, which have a real
influence within the physical organisation and which express
themselves in real effects; so that, as a result of purely occult
observation, we are obliged to speak of a real action of the
soul upon the human organism. These real effects in the finer
processes will, during the next few decades, reveal themselves
gradually and ultimately become entirely accessible to the
more refined methods of science, even to external investigation. There will then be an end to that opposition which,
arising not out of the facts of science but obviously out of
certain preconceived theories with reference to these facts,
combats such affirmations as may be based upon occult
knowledge.

Now we have also pointed out that what we look upon as
a conscious activity of the ego is after all only *one* part of
man's being; and that, below the threshold of what enters in
this manner within the horizon of our consciousness there
are processes which occur in the subconsciousness, and which
are held back from our consciousness, by means of the
sympathetic nervous system. We have been able to indicate
from various points of view that these processes which
take place below the level of consciousness have also a
certain kind of connection with our ego. We have said,
with regard to the most unconscious part of us, our bony
system, that it is organised throughout in such a way as to be
able to give to the instrument of the conscious ego the basis
for an ego. Thus, out of the unconscious, an ego-organisation
arises to meet the conscious ego-organisation. Man is thus
divided, as it were, into two parts: from one direction the
conscious ego-organisation works into the organism, and
from the other there flows into man the *unconscious* ego-

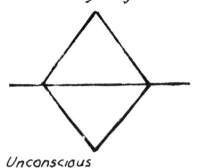

Conscious ego-organisation organisation. We have seen that the blood-system and the bony system really form a certain antithesis; they act like opposite poles. The blood in its inner activity responds to and follows, as an instrument, the activity of the ego; on the contrary, Unconscious that part which is organised ego-organisation as the other pole of the ego so that the ego is able to express itself in the blood, namely the bony system, withdraws itself from the quickened inner life of the ego to such an extent that the ego has no consciousness of anything that goes on within this bony system, and the processes here take their course below the surface of what goes on in the actually conscious ego-life. These are processes, therefore, which correspond to our ego-activity yet at the same time are as truly *dead* as our blood-processes are *living*; and they are, as a matter of fact, only one portion of those processes which remain unconscious to the ego, and which only gradually rise more and more up into the conscious.

If we study this bony system thoughtfully with regard to its functioning as a whole in the human organism, we cannot but be struck by the fact that it really withdraws itself, as it were, from all conscious life, and that it does this to a greater degree than any of the other systems of organs. If at the same time we go on from this bony system to the other organic systems, for example, to that inner cosmic system of the liver and spleen, the heart and lungs, etc, we are compelled to affirm that the processes within these systems are also to a very high degree withdrawn from our conscious life, although not so completely as those in our bony system. We certainly need to give far less conscious thought and attention to our bony system than to these other organs just mentioned. Some of these latter make known very clearly in their functions, in the case of some people at any rate, that they do reach up into the plane of consciousness. Just as beings which dwell in the waters of the ocean push the waves up to the surface, so does much of what goes on in the heart or the other organs belonging to these systems push its way up into our conscious life. We know how hypochondriacs, to their own injury, naturally, are partly aware of these things even though in an entirely different way, to be sure, from that in which they actually take place below. I do not here refer at all to the fact that a certain degree of illness may be developed in these organs, for then it is, of course, something quite different which causes the person to become conscious of them. I mean that one need not come anywhere near that border-line which a healthy man may designate as "bordering on being ill." This border-line, unfortunately, gets very much displaced nowadays, to the great injury of humanity. We know, at the same time, that we are protected from becoming conscious of what goes on below by means of the sympathetic nervous system opposing these inner processes.

If we recognise in the bony system something that so builds man up, as regards his form and structure, that the blood-system can be a fitting instrument within it for the ego, we must have a certain understanding, after what has just been stated, of the fact that the other organs, for example, those organs belonging to the inner cosmic system, are in their turn in a certain sense in the process of growing to meet the conscious life of man which is destined to unfold itself as the flowering of man's organisation. We must see clearly that all of these organs, although they are not permeated with fully conscious life, do nevertheless contain that something which is growing toward our soul-life, just as we have seen that our bony system is growing toward the ego-life.

Now we must ask ourselves at this point: to what extent then, does this inner system, which we may designate as an inner cosmic system, grow toward man's conscious soul-life? If, on the one hand, it is clear to us that in the bony system we have our surest support for what brings order into the blood-system, enabling this blood-system to evolve into an instrument of our ego, and its separate parts to occupy the right places, we must admit, on the other hand, that the function of the bony system as the fundamental basis of our organisation is such that it also supports, at the same time, those organs constituting an inner cosmic system, and brings them into the right position. For the same thing in the bony system which is advantageous to the blood-system is also advantageous to these organs. And, if we make even a purely external study of these organs, we shall be especially struck by the fact that we can discover nothing in them, either in their disposition or even in their form, that is so intimately related to the outer limits of man's form as is the bony system.

We have something then, in man, which we may describe by saying that the bony system is the foundation, and whatever is disposed around it can be thus disposed only because it gives man his basic form. If we recognise in man's skin his external boundary, we must affirm that to a great extent this external skin-boundary is already forecast by the whole structure of the bony system, a fact which led to Goethe saying in such impressive words, nor merely aesthetically impressive but wonderfully fine also as a scientific expression: "There is nothing in the skin which is not also in the bones." That is to say, in the external skin-formation, by means of which man's being is expressed in form, is demonstrated what is already there as a model in the bony system. This we cannot say with regard to our inner cosmic system. Yet, on the other hand, the fact that the functioning of this inner cosmic system thrusts itself up into lower levels of consciousness shows us that it has some-thing to do with our astral body; for the astral body is the bearer of consciousness. And the reason why the astral body as the bearer of consciousness does not consciously experience what goes on in this inner cosmic system is that the sympathetic nerve-system holds it back. This we have already mentioned.

We must affirm, therefore, that this inner cosmic system does not appear to be an expression of the subconscious self, that self which is to be found as a model deep down in the foundation of man's being but, rather, that it is so incorporated in us through the universal cosmic process, that its relation to our astral body is similar to that other relation which enables the human form as expressed in the bony system to offer a basis for the most comprehensive form of the ego. We may say, therefore, that in the bony system, but deep down in the unconscious, we have an already highly developed pattern of the human ego; and that in what we call our inner cosmic system we have the pattern of our so-called astral body. It is important to keep this disposition clearly in mind: the bony system serves as a basic model for all that we call our ego—naturally, we mean this in the sense in which we are here discussing it —and the inner cosmic system for what we call our astral body.

Of course this inner cosmic system, in its entire organ-isation, since it still lies almost wholly *below* the level of consciousness, does not in any way derive from the conscious soul-life but is implanted in us, through our external organisation, out of the cosmos. This means that something we may call a *cosmic astral* element merges with us in such a way that it expresses itself in our inner cosmic system. In our bony system, there is merged into our whole organism, here again out of our whole environment, that which the cosmic process is able to bestow upon us. Since this is connected with the entire form of our physical organisation, we must say that this bony system is really, as a result, the basis of our physical body so far as this appears before us within the boundary of its physical form. A macrocosmic element or, to put it plainly, a cosmic system, which has given us the physical form we have as human beings, has been deposited in our bony system; a macrocosmic astral world-system is deposited in our inner cosmic system. The ego, in so far as it appears as a conscious ego, has the blood-system for its instrument; but, in so far as it is forecast as form, as structure, there lies at its foundation a cosmic force-system which presses into the ego-organisation, into the firm ego-formation, and which sets its deepest imprint in our bony system.

Let us grasp the matter clearly from still another point of view. We know that everything which manifests itself in the ego as a thought-element comes to expression through a kind of salt-deposit, if I may use such an expression as this; for you can well understand that ordinary expressions are scarcely to be found for things which are not in the least understood by the ordinary human consciousness, yet are known by clairvoyant consciousness to be a process of salt-deposit of the finest possible kind. In our bony system, in which our ego was modelled beforehand out of the cosmos, and where it has its firmest support so that the whole organism possesses this support, there also we may accordingly expect to find that a "salt-deposit" must have been forecast for us as thinking beings, and here again through the physical process of salt-depositing. In other words we may expect to find salt-deposits in the bony system. And, in actual fact, we do find that the bones consist of phosphate of lime and calcium carbonate, that is, of salt-deposits.

Thus we have, here again, two opposite poles. Man is a thinking being, and it is the thought-process that makes him inwardly a stable being (for, in a certain sense, our thought-system is our inner bony system; we have definite, sharply-outlined thoughts: and though our feelings are more or less indefinite, wavering, and different in each one of us, the thought-systems are inserted in stable form in the feeling system). Now whereas these stable insertions of thought in the conscious life manifest themselves through a sort of animated, mobile process of salt-depositing, that which prepares the way for these in the bony system, giving them the right support, expresses itself in the fact that the macrocosm out of its own formative processes so builds up our bony system that a part of its nature consists of deposited salts. These deposited salts of the bony system are the quiescent element in us: they are the opposite pole to those inner vital activities which are at play in the process of salt-depositing corresponding to the principle of thought. Thus we are made capable of thought through influences acting from two sides upon our organisation: from one side *un-consciously* through the fact that our bony system is built up within us; from the other side *consciously* in that we ourselves bring about, after the model of our bone-building process, conscious processes which manifest themselves as of like nature in our organism, and of which we may say that they are inwardly active processes. For the salt that is here formed must again at once be dissolved by sleep, must be got rid of, for otherwise it would induce destructive processes, causing dissolution. Thus we have processes that begin with the deposition of salt and then are followed by destructive processes, constituting a sort of reactionary process. In the re-dissolving of the deposits, beneficent sleep acts upon us in the way we need, to the end that we may ever anew develop conscious thought in our fully awake life of day.

If we proceed further, we can understand that all processes which occur within the human organism must take place between these two polar-extremes of salt-formation. We are here dealing with the process of salt formation in the spiritual sense, but this must be conceived as I have to-day explained it. It will not do simply to say: "Thinking is a process of salt-formation"; for people will then imagine what is now popularly conceived by the layman as the process of salt-formation; and then it will be easy to say that Spiritual Science maintains absurdities and nonsense. Between these processes, which must be conceived only in the sense we have indicated, there lie all the other processes to which we have called attention. For, if we have salt-formation occurring in a vitally active thought-process, and the opposite pole of this in the salt-formation of our bony system which has to a certain extent come to rest, we can likewise affirm that we have all through our organs the opposite pole of what we may designate as the liquefying process, as inner coagulation, as a flocculent process, albumen-like insertions or something similar. In this case, again, it is not to be found only under the influence of our own feeling life, which takes its course more in the depths of the soul, but from the bone-building process also. In this connection we must say that all processes which are more inward in character (which belong more to the soul and to the central processes of our organism than

does the bone-forming process) are involved in the unconscious liquefying processes and thickening of substances
which are formed and deposited as we have described. Now
the first thing we come upon here is something in which the
bone-building process is actually involved, namely, those
liquefying processes to be found in what is mingled with the
bone-salts as the so-called bone-glue. In these processes
the other pole of our bony system participates and thereby
meets that which forms the physical correlative of our
feeling process. The process connected with the will impulse
expresses itself in a warmth process, an inner warming
process, so to speak. Processes of combustion, the formation
of combinations which we call inner processes of oxidation,
occur throughout our entire organisation; and, in so far as
these go on below the threshold of consciousness and have
nothing to do with the conscious life, will-impulses and the
like, they belong to that other part of our organisation which
is shut off by the corresponding organs and is susceptible to
influence from the subconscious life.

The human being is thus protected inwardly on one side
by a part of his organism in which these processes take their
course much as they do outwardly in the macrocosm; and on
the other side his protection is such that these processes
are connected with his soul-processes, and are of a finer kind
as has been explained. And so these physiological processes
take place in our organism, salt-forming, liquefying, and
warmth producing processes, which are the result of our
conscious life; and others which take place outside our
conscious life, in such a way that they furnish the basis for
what prepares itself beforehand in the human organism in
order that the processes adapted to the conscious life may
take place. Our organism as a whole is thus a texture woven
of those processes which we must describe as belonging in

part to our conscious life and in part to the unconscious. It is an extraordinarily significant fact that our organism actually does represent a union formed out of two polar opposites: that processes of coarser nature take place in such a way that they radiate into the organism, as it were, out of the macrocosm; and that, on the other hand, there are processes of a finer sort which arise out of our conscious life.

Now, since the organism is a single *whole* and all these parts interpenetrate and influence one another, the situation in this organism, as we have it to-day, is such that all these processes likewise play into one another and that we cannot so separate them one from another as to fix definite bounddaries between them. One process plays into another. You need consider only the blood, the most vitally active and finest element. In this element you may perceive a stimulator of the salt-forming process, the process of condensation of a fluid, and the warming process. And likewise in all the systems of organs you may perceive how these processes take their course, and how they are stimulated. Let us therefore say, for example, that when we take nutritive substances from without into our digestive canal these nutritive substances have within themselves what I have called "external vital activity." They pass through what we may call the first stage of filtering by being taken in and digested by the stomach and what pertains to it; and they are then worked up in more special details by the inner cosmic system, and conveyed to where they can also nourish the finest instrument of the organism, the blood. Thus it is the inner cosmic system which undertakes this first filtering of the nutritive substances, which then have to be conveyed to all the other systems. At the same time, since we have recognised a *series of stages* in the organic systems of man, we may readily conceive that the most delicate system of all, the blood, must take into itself the most completely filtered vital activities of the nutriment, and that, when anything whatever enters into the blood, it contains by that time only the very least possible amount of that inner vital activity that was in the substances when they were taken in by the stomach. When the substances enter into the stomach they still contain a considerable part of their own nature and essential character, their own vital activity. But when once they are in the blood they must have surrendered all this, in so far as they are nutritive substances that have been conducted into the blood, and must have become something new. The blood is thus something which shields inwardly, in the highest degree, all its processes, something that carries on its processes in the greatest measure independently of the outer world. Such is the blood from the *one* point of view.

But we have already indicated that this blood is like a tablet which is equally exposed on its two sides, exposed, that is, to impressions coming from both directions. It is turned on the one side to the subconscious processes in the deeper regions of the human organism, where the nutritive substances, after going through filtering processes, come up and force their way to the blood. The influence of every-thing occurring there is diminished by the sympathetic nervous system, so that it does not reach our consciousness. And the *other* side of the tablet must be turned by the blood to the experiences of the conscious life of the soul. Not only the unconscious activities of the ego, which work up from the bony system, but also the conscious soul-activites, belonging to the other ego, must penetrate into the blood. They must be able to metamorphose themselves by the time they reach the blood, in order that they then may become the expression of what we have about us in our environment as material world; for of course that which is woven into the plant world as ether-body, for example, is not visible to normal consciousness. It is the physical world, first of all, that we have around us; and, for the normal consciousness, we ourselves belong only to the physical world. Thus we expose this other side of our "blood-tablet" to the material world which then becomes the content of our consciousness. The entire soul-life, as it is stimulated into thought through the impressions of the material world and as it flames into feelings and is stirred into impulses of will, must find its instrument in the blood-system in so far as it is conscious ego-life.

And what does this signify? Nothing other than this: that not only are we able to have in our blood that into which the nutritive substances have been changed, when they have been driven upward from the subconscious and filtered to the point where they may lead a life of their own in the blood, shielded from all macrocosmic laws; but also that there must be inscribed on the other side of the tablet of the blood all that occurs in the material realm, in the lifeless matter of the material world, which is known to us through sense-impressions and appears to our consciousness, at first, in the form of everything that can make impressions. For whatever goes to make up life can become known to the normal consciousness only through combinations of physical sense-impressions. In reality it becomes known only through the next higher supersensible member, the ether-body. Thus the blood must be capable of being also related to the physical-sensible world just as this immediately surrounds us.

We may, accordingly, expect to find that something is incorporated into the blood which, we might say, does not manifest itself there as if it were due to the influence of processes working up from the lower depths of our nature, but rather as if it were due to the influence of external macrocosmic laws and vital activities. We must have in our blood, therefore, something that is similar in character and action to direct external processes, which take their course outside of us in the same way in which they gradually come later to take their course within our organism. That is, there must be physical, chemical, inorganic processes which take their course within our blood, which are necessary to enable our ego to take part in the physical world. Thus we shall have to seek in the blood for processes wherein substances can act through their physical-sensible character, in accordance with what they are in the macrocosm. And this we do find, as a matter of fact, in that something is presented to us in the red corpuscles which shows us that it is just *beginning to live,* and is at the point where it passes over to the state of lifelessness. And from the other side of the tablet something is incorporated into the blood which we may call a process easily comparable to an external process of combustion. In short we have in the blood, disposed on the other side, and recognisable even physically, everything that makes man a physical-sensible being through the fact that in the blood he has an instrument for his ego which is living in this physical-sensible world.

Thus, even concerning the organisation of the blood, physical chemical research itself can show us how significant, how illuminating, occult premises may be for what is presented to direct inquiry into the physiology of man.

From all the foregoing we may say that we have in the human organism, in the first place, processes which are stimulated by the blood-process in so far as this is related to the outside world, and which constitute physical-sensible processes of the outside world; but that we have also other processes which reach as far as the blood-system from the other direction, and are fitted into this system after they have been filtered to the last degree. Only when we clearly perceive this will the blood appear to us the truly important organ it is. We shall see that it has on the one hand turned its entire being, so to speak, toward life in the very lowest and most basic forms that we know round about us, so that it almost becomes a material substance which tends continually to evoke physical chemical processes in order to be able to serve as an instrument for the ego; and on the other hand that it is the most completely shielded of substances, which carries on inner processes that could not be carried on anywhere else, because everything which is pre-requisite to those processes is dependent upon all the other processes that fit themselves into the processes of the blood. In other words the *finest* and *highest* processes which are stimulated out of the depths of our organism unite, within the circuit of our blood, with the other, the physical chemical processes, which obey the laws of the external world. In no other physical substance does the material world meet quite as immediately with something quite different — something that requires the activity of supersensible systems of forces for its existence — as in our blood. This is not manifested in the physical world in any other substance as in the blood which permeates man's organism. In fact, this blood is something in which the lowliest that man can see in processes around him is combined with the loftiest that can take on organic form within his nature.

It will be entirely clear to us, therefore, that in these blood-processes we have before us something which, if it becomes irregular, unrhythmical, must cause irregularities in the greatest measure in our entire organism. And since the blood is the expression of the whole collection of organic processes we shall have to consider carefully, in connection with irregularities of the blood, where abnormal phenomena are manifest, difficult to distinguish individually, to which particular course of processes we must attribute these irregularities. If, for instance, they are to be found in those processes in the blood-channels which follow the pattern of physical chemical processes in the outer world, we shall then have to be quite clear that these irregularities, which we must learn to recognise and not confuse them, must be dealt with from the side of consciousness, in so far as this consciousness is associated with the physical plane. And here a field is opened, a therapeutic field, which we may think of as one by way of which we shall learn to see whether certain irregularities in the circulation of the blood are connected with such processes as we may call in the true sense of the term *physical chemical* processes. We shall then be able to intervene by means of such external impressions and appropriate control of external sense-impressions as we can evoke in dealing with a human being, in this case such external impressions as can produce physical chemical processes, that is, through everything which we can convey to the physical organism from without. By this we mean not so much the soul and spiritual impressions we can employ, though these are also included, as all those especially which we can effect through a control of the breathing process, through watching over the breathing process and also over the reciprocal action of the human organism and the external world through the skin.

Then again we can also see in the blood-organism the most delicate organic processes working from the other direction. And we shall have to understand, with reference to this blood-organism, that it represents the third stage in the refinement of our nutritive substances. If the blood-organism, because it evokes those delicate processes of salt forming, liquefaction and warmth under the influence of external impressions, is thereby predetermined from without in its physical chemical course by the soul-processes themselves, we may ask how this process as a blood-process is determined from within. We must distinguish the function belonging to the blood by reason of the fact that it is blood; but we must also understand that it needs to be nourished just like any other organ: we must consider it in the same way as any other organ that needs to be nourished. And on the other hand we must also recognise it as the organ standing at the highest stage of organic activity. With regard to this activity we must consider especially what we call the inner support of human life. The blood, which is the opposite extreme, so to speak, from the bony system, must be most of all protected in order that in our thinking it may create, as the instrument of thought in so far as this thought has ego-consciousness— that it may be able to create the process we have called the deposition of salt. This protection must proceed from the blood itself; therefore the blood must above everything be capable of calling forth, spiritually as it were, a spiritual bony system, must be able itself to cause the process of salt-forming. This is a task to which the blood must so devote itself that it can be independent of the other organs, and need only receive from the other organs the least possible support for its own work. Least of all do the vital activities of the other organs play into this salinating process of the blood, so that in respect to this process of salt deposition, in relation to thought, the blood intensifies the inner existence of man.

And how can we fail to recognise this, since our thought is the most inward thing we have, that in which we most completely interiorise ourselves to our normal consciousness? Whereas in our feelings we are, to our normal consciousness, at the border-line between the inner and the outer, and in our will-impulses we come into such strong contact with the outer world that under ordinary circumstances the human being no longer recognises himself in his will-impulses! Man recognises himself always in his thoughts, but not in his impulses of will. This may be seen from the fact that there has been so much controversy in the world over the question of the freedom or absence of freedom of the human will, as well as over its other qualities. In our thought-system, which has its physical correlative in a process of salt deposition, we have the innermost aspect of what the blood has to accomplish as an instrument of the ego. And since the process of salt deposition must be completely interiorised and protected against the other organs, this capacity of the blood may be most of all hindered by abnormalities within it. When we note that the blood is so hindered that it no longer manifests its capacity in this direction, we must understand that it needs to be stimulated to that sort of of activity which has fallen below a certain border-line in its own particular life.

But the other situation may come about, in which the inner vital activity of an organ, let us say, in this case, the organ of the blood, whose inner vital activity is destined to develop a life of its own, passes beyond a certain limit, exercises unduly this life of its own. Among all occurring human irregularities this is by far the most serious, since it has most of all to do with cases of illness. Only seldom have we to deal with the opposite condition. It is generally the case that certain parts of the inner organisation are too little protected and therefore too intensely stimulated. When the blood shows itself to be most highly stimulated, when it shows an excessive tendency to develop this activity, it then becomes necessary to counteract this. We can remedy this by introducing the appropriate vital activities from without. In other words, we co-operate in the process of salination, of salt-depositing, by the therapeutic introduction of such substances as contribute to bring it about. This leads us at once to see that a kind of system may be introduced into the way in which we have to deal with the irregularities of our organism.

We may now proceed still further in this direction. When the organs of our inner astral world, our inner cosmic system, spleen, liver, gall-bladder, etc., are excessive in their inner vital activity, as regards the special character of their functions, how can we deal with them? Here we must call to our minds, above all, that these organs are appointed to a work which goes on all the way up to the circulation of the blood; that they have to prepare beforehand, so to speak, the entire organism, have to direct the nutritive substances as far as the blood by taking them over as they are conveyed into the digestive canal and leading them, with their vital activities transformed, to the blood-system. Hence they are the mediators between these two systems. Just as the blood-system manifests the greatest quickening of inner activity, in so far as it constitutes the thought-system, so it takes on an activity that manifests a connection with our life of feeling, in the way we described when we said that in the process of condensation, of inner liquefaction, the blood-system is supported by what radiates from our inner cosmic system. The blood is left almost entirely to itself in so far as it is the instrument of the element of thought in us; it is stimulated by what radiates upward, by that in which the organs of the inner cosmic system participate, through their own action— so that we have here to call attention to an activity which goes even beyond the individual life of the blood and directs us to the individual life of these organs belonging to the inner cosmic system.

Now, when the functions of these organs, liver, gall-bladder, kidneys, lungs, and the rest, develop too intense a vital activity, an overflow of life, we are then concerned with the question how we may in similar fashion deal therapeutically with these processes. We have to paralyse the inner vital activities by introducing something which is adapted to maintain the activity, the vitality, of external cosmic life and thus to paralyse the exaggerated inner vitality. Just as we combat the excessive inner vital activities of the blood, paralyse them, so to speak, by introducing salt-containing substances, so we may also reduce the excessive activity of these organs by introducing substances which develop their own inner vital activities and work in opposition to those of the organs concerned.

Thus the question now arises for us, how we can work on these organs and also on the lowest organs, which have a still lower function: on those digestive organs, namely, which have to do with the preliminary preparation of the nutritive substances for the inner cosmic system. In other words, how shall we deal with the individual organic systems when we consider their gradual upbuilding, stage by stage? In to-morrow's lecture we shall answer the question, "How does the picture of a diseased organ appear to us in the light of occult physiology?" And we shall also show how other organs are incorporated, for example, the system of muscles. And we shall bring our reflections to an end by showing that what confronts us in the already evolved organism is quite plainly connected with the *becoming* organism, with the human germinal life, indeed, it is precisely here that this is so very distinct, if we are able to presuppose occult principles. It will then become clear to us, quite of itself, how the remaining members participate in the work of the human physical organisation.

THE HUMAN FORM AND ITS CO-ORDINATION
OF FORCES

28th March, 1911.

It will be my task to-day to blend into a sort of picture, though naturally only a sketchy one, our reflections of the last few days regarding "occult physiology," in which the endeavour has been made to present (though in part likewise only sketchily) much that pertains to the processes of the human organisation. Through this picture it will be possible for us to have a vision of the quickening life which weaves and works throughout the human organisation. Here again our best procedure will be to start from the most common and everyday side, the reciprocal relationship between the human organisation and the outer world, our earth, in the process of taking in nutritive substances.

It is these substances, as we know, after they have been taken in and have passed through various stages of change, that are conveyed through the most diverse actions of the organs to the separate members of the human organisation, to all the individual systems constituting the physical being of man. Indeed it requires no special effort to see that, fundamentally considered, what the human organism succeeds in doing with the nutritive substances is what really makes the human being into the physical man as he stands before us in the physical world. To be sure, there is a certain difficulty in taking such a view. But anyone who is serious about the principles that have here been applied in our reflections re- garding the human being, must say to himself that everything else to be considered in connection with the human organisation, apart from this impressing of nutritive substances into the organism, is, fundamentally viewed, something supersensible, invisible, the actions of force. If you banish from your mind for a moment everything by way of nutritive substances which fills out the human organism, you retain as a physical organisation even less than a mere physical sack, if I may be permitted this trivial expression; indeed, you retain nothing whatever of a physical character. For even what exists in the form of skin and outer covering exists solely by reason of the fact that nutritive substances have been driven to particular areas of action of super-sensible forces. Cancel then from your reckoning the nutritive substances and what is produced out of them, and you have to conceive the human organism as a system of supersensible forces working behind it in such a way that these same nutritive substances may be conveyed in all directions.

If you hold to this thought you will see that one thing must be presupposed before any nutritive substance whatever, even the tiniest particle, is taken in; for these substances could not be taken in from the outer world in just any chance form and conveyed into just any being, in order that those processes should occur which do occur in the human organism. It must be, then, that this human organism confronts the very first nutritive substances taken in with an inner co-ordination of forces coming from the spiritual worlds; the organism must really be "man," as such, in this inner co-ordination of forces. In all occultism, this which first confronts the purely physical matter that is to fill out the human being (and which must, therefore, always be conceived supersensibly) is called, in the most comprehensive sense of the expression, "the human form." If, therefore, you descend to the nethermost boundary of the human organisation, you have to conceive the primary supersensible human form which, as a force-system born out of the supersensible worlds, is destined, not like a sack or a physical bag but as something superphysical, supersensible, to take in what alone renders possible the physical-sensible manifestation of the human being. Only by reason of the fact that this supersensible form incorporates the nutritive matter does the human organism become a material organism, something that our eyes can behold and our hands can grasp. That which thus confronts the external nutritive substances is called "form" in accordance with the law that is operative throughout the whole of nature, an identical law termed the "principle of form." Even though you descend to the crystal, you find that the substances which enter into it, if they are to become what is manifest as the crystal, must be seized as it were by form-principles, which in this case are the principles of crystallisation. Take for example kitchen salt or sodium chloride: here you have, according to our present-day physics, the physical substances chlorine and sodium, a gas and a mineral. You will readily see that these two substances, prior to their entrance into the entity which lays hold upon them in such a way that, in their chemical union, they appear crystallised into a cube, have nothing in them that can indicate to us such a form-principle. Before they enter into this form-principle they possess nothing in common, but they are seized upon and yoked together by this form-principle and there is then produced this physical body, kitchen salt. They presuppose this, we may say. And in the same way everything which enters the human organism as nutritive substance presupposes the lowest supersensible essence, the supersensible *form.*

Now, when the nutritive substances enter into that sphere which, by means of this form-principle, is externally bounded as the human being, they are first taken in by the alimentary canal. When they are thus taken in, from the moment they enter the mouth, one might say, they at once undergo the very first change, indeed the alimentary canal itself causes a metamorphosis. This could not be produced if there were not present as an integral part of the human organism, something which would so metamorphose these nutritive substances—entirely neutral in relation to each other when first taken in and possessing no living inter-relationship—that they are evoked into *life*. We must think of the metamorphosis of the nutritive substances in their passage through the human alimentary canal as similar to that of plants when they take their nutritive substances from the soil, although, of course, the process is quite different in the human being because it takes place at a different stage. We must picture to ourselves a nutritional stream, taken in by the life-process, or, as we say in occultism, by the ether-body. The moment the nutritive substances enter the human organism they are worked over by the ether-body: that is, the ether-body first provides for their metamorphosis, for their being made a component part of the inner vital activities of the organism. We thus have to look upon this nearest supersensible member of the human being, the ether-body, as the stimulator of the first process of metamorphosis in the nutritive substances. After these substances are sufficiently metamorphosed to have been taken up into the life-process, we must understand clearly that they are still further worked over—in just that sense, and in the same way, which we have described in the preceding lectures. They must be still further adapted to the human organism, be so worked over that they are able little by little to serve those organs which are the manifestation of the higher supersensible principles, the astral body and the ego. In short, the work of the higher processes clearly is to send their own peculiar kind of inner vital activity down as far as these metamorphosed nutritive substances as they are when they have come through the oesophagus, the stomach, the intestines, etc. At this point the nutritional stream, in so far as it has been metamorphosed by the alimentary canal alone, is confronted by those seven inner organs already known to us which represent, as we say, the inner cosmic system of man. To sum up, the nutritive substances are taken in, at once metamorphosed in the most diverse ways in the alimentary canal, and then confronted by the liver, kidneys, gall-bladder, spleen, heart, lungs, etc.

If we further understand that these organs are designed through their corresponding force-systems to work further over the nutritive substances, we may say with regard to the meaning of this metamorphosis that, if the nutritional stream were worked over only to the extent to which this occurs in the alimentary canal, man would have to lead a plant existence; for he would not have attained to the formation of such organs in the physical world as could become the instruments of his higher capacities. Thus the seven organs further metamorphose the nutritional stream, and what they do is prevented by the sympathetic nervous system from entering human consciousness. We have consequently, in the sympathetic nervous system and the seven organs, that which confronts the nutritional stream.

We have now gone far in penetrating from the outer into the inner side of the human organism. For everything that goes on within there, as the mutual concern of the seven organs, is something that could never go on anywhere else in our terrestrial world; and it can take place here only because this inner world is shut off from the outer world, and because its activity is therefore prepared beforehand by the alimentary canal. Here in our studies we stand within the interior of man's organism.

And here we must take note of something peculiar. Now

that we are within this organism we find that it must again inwardly organise and differentiate itself. For the performance of its manifold undertakings it must work as a multiplicity of organs; and it is precisely for these inner functions that a very great deal is needed. Whatever more is now to be attained can be attained only in the following manner; and we shall understand this if we first imagine how it would be if there were only this metamorphosis of the nutritional stream by means of the seven organs, the inner cosmic system, and imagine also that this process were concealed from our consciousness by the sympathetic nervous system. That would mean that man would never be able to unfold into a being possessed of consciousness; he would never have even the dimmest form of the consciousness which he now possesses. For everything occurring there is withheld from him. A connection must be established between this system of organs, built into him, as it were, from without, and everything else in the interior of the human organism. This connection is actually established through the fact that everything provided by the nutritive process as a whole causes the entire form of the organism to be interwoven with what we call *tissue*, in the broadest sense of the term. Tissue, one of the very simplest forms of organisation, is woven through all the separate members of the human entity. And out of this tissue the most diverse organs form themselves. Certain kinds of tissue, for instance, change themselves in such a way that when they have added to their composition other special kinds of cells they are transformed into muscles. Then again, other kinds change themselves by hardening and, through the appropriation of suitable substances, by depositing bone-cells. Thus, in the single organs which form themselves so as together to fill out the form of the human organism as a whole, we must think of something as underlying this organism: in other words, we must think of tissues woven throughout the body, and active everywhere, bringing forth out of themselves the individual organs.

But this tissue, no matter how much it might grow, and no matter how many individual organs it might put forth out of itself, would still constitute basically nothing more than something plant-like; for the essential nature of the plant lies in the fact that the plant-entity grows, that it produces organs out of itself and so on. Since however in the case of man we are to go beyond the plant nature, an entirely new element must present itself by means of which man becomes capable of adding to what exists in plant-life, that which elevates him above it. That is, man must add *consciousness*, the simplest form at first, that dim consciousness by which he is aware of his own inner life. So long as a living being does not consciously share in its own inner life, is not in position to mirror its own inner life and thus share it consciously, we cannot say that it has risen above the plant nature. Only through this fact that it does not merely have "life" in itself, but mirrors the flow of its inner life and raises it to conscious life, does any being rise above the plant-like state. It is at first, then, an inner experience, an experience of the inner life-processes.

How does experience come into existence?

We have already forecast a conception of this. In the earlier lectures we have shown that experience comes about through the *processes of excretion*.[1] For this reason we shall have to look for the basis of inner experience, of that dim experience of consciousness which permeates the inner life-processes, in the processes of excretion. We shall have to presume that everywhere, out of tissues, out of all that

1 See footnote on p. 103.

underlies the human organisation, processes of excretion are taking place. And these excretory processes again do manifest themselves when we observe the human body externally and see how substances from all parts of the tissue and the organs are continually being taken up by what we call the *lymph vessels*, which permeate the whole organism as another kind of system parallel to that of the blood. From all regions of the human organism those excretions which mediate that dim inner experience enter this system. Thus we might in abstract thought banish from our minds for the moment the whole system of the blood, in which case indeed we should conceive the tissue as though it possessed no blood-like character. This is quite conceivable, and the fluids in the lower organisms do actually have such an appearance. We should thus have to imagine our blood-process as one higher than that which takes place when excretions from every region of the organism enter into the lymph-channels which, we know, accompany the blood-channels which join them later. In these excretions the human being dimly feels, as it were, his animal existence in the physical body, dimly mirrors his organisation. And, just as everything is held back from consciousness by the sympathetic nervous system which comes to life through the digestive and nutritional process as far as the seven organs, just so through the reflection of the activity of the sympathetic nervous system, through the association and reciprocal action between this system and the lymph-channels, there is formed for the present-day human being a dim consciousness which is outshone by the clear day-consciousness of the ego. This dim consciousness is, as it were, the obverse side of that consciousness which utilises the sympathetic nervous system as its instrument. It is outshone, as a powerful light outshines a feeble light, by all that lives in our souls under the influence of the *ego*.

Now let us suppose for a moment that we had evolved the human organisation *only to this point,* to the formation of the bodily tissues and the first organs that must be formed in order to render possible all these processes; for you can see that certain muscles have to be incorporated to enable such processes to take place as, for example, the secretions into the lymph-channel. A man thus organised would be able to maintain a dim consciousness of his inner life in the physical world, mediated to him by means of his organism; but he would not be able to attain to that ego-consciousness which can be present only when man does not merely have an *inner* experience of himself as a being, but also opens himself to the external world. It is this opening again outward, so to speak, to which we must here call attention.

We have already spoken indeed of this reopening outward. We have shown how the human being opens himself again to the outside world in his breathing and so forth, in order to enter into direct contact with the physical world. We may now go even further, since we have seen how hard it is to apply ordinary concepts to these things, and say that, so long as we confine ourselves to the inner man, we can go only as far as the alimentary canal; for, inasmuch as the extensions of the seven organs reach into the alimentary canal and show themselves there (the liver empties through the gall-bladder into the duodenum) and show their influence in the digestion, we at once disclose, through the impact of this inner cosmic system on the alimentary canal, something which amounts to the reopening of ourselves to the outer world. Thus it is really an opening outward when the human being declares himself ready to receive nutritive substances from without; and hence we need reckon the inner man only as far as the boundary of the alimentary canal. Then we have also another opening outward through the breathing, on the one hand,

and on the other hand through the higher organs which serve the functions of the soul.

Thus we see how man, in so far as he has the stage of the dimly conscious inner life as something basic in him, so to speak, reopens himself in order to form a connection with the external world. Only in this way can man become an *ego-being*. For it is not merely in the process of sensing the resistance in his own inner world, in his processes of secretion, but through the fact that he opens his inner world and senses the resistance of the outer world, that he is able to evolve his ego-consciousness. Thus it is really wholly in the fact that man reopens himself outward that we find the basis for his physical egohood. At the same time, however, he must also possess the capacity to develop the organ of this egohood in the most manifold ways. And we have seen how the organ for the ego here fits itself into the circulatory course of the blood, which in fact passes through all these inner organs, in order to serve throughout the whole human organisation as an instrument for the egohood. Just as the egohood permeates soul and spirit in the whole man, so does the circulatory course of the blood physically permeate his entire organisation. And this organisation thereby evolves these two sides, so to speak: the inner human being in the seven organs, the sympathetic nervous system, the system of tissues, and predominantly in the digestive apparatus, etc.; and the other side that again opens outward, coming into connection with the outer world, a real "circulation" in the highest sense of the word.

We must now give still further attention to the individual phases of this circulation. And what concerns us here, first of all, is to follow once more the nutritional process, the taking in of nutritive substances which become a living stream in the human organism through the fact that they are taken up by the ether-body, or, rather, are grasped by the force of the ether-body. The inner cosmic system, consisting of the seven organs, then meets these substances; and it does this because, as we have seen, the human being would otherwise not rise above a plant-existence. The higher stage of man's being requires that these seven organs should go out to meet the digestive process. So that it really is what comes to life in the astral nature of man that works upon the nutritional stream: this stream comes from without, and that which constitutes the inner nature of man goes forth to meet and work upon it. First of all the ether-body meets the nutritional stream, and metamorphoses its substances all along the course of the digestive system; then the astral system goes forth to meet them, metamorphoses them still further, and makes them so much a part of the inner world that they more and more become inner vital activities. And now, since everything in the human organism constitutes a co-operative unity, the entire nutritional stream must in addition be taken hold of by the forces of the ego, by the blood itself. That is, the instrument of the ego must extend its activity down to where the nutritional stream is taken up. Does the blood do this? Can we verify that which occult perception compels us to affirm?

Yes, we can; for the blood is actually driven down into the organs of nutrition, just as it is into all other organs. In this nutritional organisation, as elsewhere, it goes through the entire process whereby it is capable of being the instrument of man's ego in the physical world. We know that the blood, as the instrument of the ego, passes through the transition from red blood to blue, so that here, too, it meets with resistance. Thus the ego, by means of its instrument, reaches down even to the nutritive processes, since this transformed blood, in order to be the expression of the ego, works upon almost the first beginnings of the nutritive process. This occurs through the fact that the portal *system of veins* discharges into the liver, and that out of this modified blood the gall is prepared, which then comes into direct contact with the nutritional system.

We thus have a wonderful union of the two extremes of the human organisation. The nutritional stream, on the one hand, is taken into the digestive tract and this represents the external matter which enters our physical organisation. The ego, on the other hand, together with its instrument the blood, constitutes the noblest endowment which man possesses in the terrestrial world. It establishes a direct connection with the nutritional stream in that it comes to the very end of the blood-process, and there, at the end of the blood-process, in turn brings about the preparation of something which, we may say, directly confronts the nutritional stream. In other words, the gall is prepared by the instrument of the ego, the blood, through the roundabout way of the liver; and in the gall the ego opposes the nutritional stream. For at this point the activity of the blood has come to an end and, before acting upon the nutritional stream, it is able to prepare the gall.

Here we see the one working downward, as it were, into the other. And whoever has the will to do so can see in this very fact something that leads in a wonderful way into many, many mysteries of the human organisation. He can follow these processes still further, including abnormal processes, which take their course, for example, in a reverse discharge, a congesting and reverse discharging of the gall into the blood. He might thus quite easily form an opinion about "jaundice," for example, its cause and effect; but it would take us too far afield if we were also to discuss such things as this to-day.

Thus we see how the seven organs reach as an actual fact down into the action of the ether-body and have taken into themselves, from above, the influence of the ego. In the gall we have the ego setting itself in direct opposition to the nutritional stream. If, now, the gall is to meet this nutritional stream, which has already become a living stream in the alimentary canal, it must itself likewise meet it as a *living* substance; otherwise a truly continuous process could not come about. The gall must be enabled, as a living substance, to meet the nutritional stream. This occurs through the fact that the very organ in which this gall is formed is one of the seven organs of the inner cosmic system, which vitalise the inner life of man in order that it may as inner life meet the outer life. We pass from the gall-bladder back into the liver itself, and the liver in turn we find connected with the spleen.

When we more closely observe the liver, the gall-bladder, the spleen (this follows quite naturally out of our previous reflections, for the spleen has been fairly accurately considered in this connection and used as an example) we must affirm that it is these organs that directly confront the nutritional stream and so metamorphose it that it is capable of advancing to the higher stages of the human organisation, and also of supplying those organs which open themselves to the external world. Those which open outward are the heart (through the lungs) and, of course, the alimentary canal itself; but, most of all, the organs in the head which serve as the organs of the senses.

We must now understand clearly that all inner perception, all inner experience, must have something to do with processes of excretion. It is for this reason that we have given special consideration also to these excretory processes. Liver, gall-bladder, and spleen have nothing to do directly with processes of excretion; the fact that they secrete their own nutritive substances is a different matter; but they do not excrete anything with respect to the organisation as a whole. They signify the ascending life, which turns away from a mere being alive and directs itself to the organisation of consciousness. Since, however, the heart is added as a fourth member to this organisation, and since the heart opens itself to the outer world, man attains through this opening outward his ego-consciousness. Yet he would not be in a position to experience this ego otherwise than merely as something which faces the outer world. He would not be able to bring this outward-looking ego into relationship with what he experiences by means of his inner organs as a dim corporeal life within him. He must add to the secretional processes of the inner organisation still another process which makes possible for him an experiencing of his inner being by that ego which has its instrument in the blood. At first man experiences his inner life only in a dim consciousness and we have seen how this manifests itself in the organisation through the fact that the processes of excretion are taken up by the lymph-ducts from the liver, the gall-bladder, and the spleen. In the same way something must be excreted from the blood, if man is to rise to a really conscious ego. And it is in this excretion that he becomes aware that, as an inner entity, he confronts the outer world. If man did not have these inner excretional processes he would, in his experiences of inner life, so face the outer world that he would inwardly lose himself; or he would at most experience dim inner processes but would not know what is outside him, he would not know that what is inhaling the air and taking in nutritive substances is the same as the being which is working in him. It is possible for him to know this through the fact that he excretes the modified blood through the lungs, in the form of carbonic acid gas; and that, through the kidneys, he excretes the metamorphosed substances which must be removed from the blood in order that he may have an inner perception of his own entity.

Thus we find our assertion justified, that the organs which represent an ascending process, the liver, the gall-bladder, the spleen, as well as those representing in a certain sense a descending process, the lungs and the kidneys (although the lungs, in that they open themselves to the outer world, are at the same time the means of an ascending process; the individual organs are constantly in living reciprocal relationship, and we must not establish any hard and fast classification) we see how all these seven members of the inner human cosmic system are bound up with man's inner experience, and with the way in which he opens himself to the outer world. These seven members completely metamorphose, on the one hand, the vital activities peculiar to the nutritive substances into inner vital activities; and with these metamorphosed substances they provide for the human organism. They make it possible for man to reopen himself to the outer world. But, in addition to this, they bring it about that what he evolves as an excessively strong inner vital activity, which would not harmonise with the vital activity that penetrates into him from without, is brought into balance with this outer vital activity by being thrown off through the excretional processes of the lungs and the kidneys. So that we have before us the complete and regular control of the inner vital activities in this inner cosmic system of man. And in fact this entire relationship manifests itself in such a way that the best picture occultism can give us is to conceive the heart standing as the *sun*, at the centre, and caring for the three bodies of the inner cosmic system which signify the upward rising and upward bearing process. In the same way in which the sun is related to Saturn, Jupiter, and Mars in the planetary system, so is the inner sun, the heart, related to Saturn, spleen; Jupiter, liver; and gall-bladder, Mars, in the human organism. I should have to speak, not for weeks but for months, if I were to explain all the reasons why the relationship of the sun to the *outer* planets of our planetary system may really be declared to be parallel, for an exact and intimate occult observation, to the relationship which the heart sustains in the human organism to the inner cosmic system, i.e., to the liver, the gall-bladder, and the spleen. For it is an absolute fact that the relationship existing in the outer cosmos has been so adopted into the organism that what goes on in the great world or macrocosm, in our solar system, is mirrored in the reciprocal action among these organs. And those processes which go on between the sun and the *inner* planets, working inwards from the sun to our earth, are again reflected in the relationship of the heart-sun to the lungs as Mercury, and to the kidneys as Venus. Thus we have in this inner human cosmic system something which mirrors the external cosmic system.

We have already indicated, how, when we delve clair-voyantly into our own inner organism we can perceive this interior of ours; and that we then cease to perceive our inner organs in the way they manifest themselves merely to the external observation of the physical eye. We then go beyond the fantastic picture of our organs conceived by external anatomy, for we rise to the observation of the real form of these organs when we bear in mind that they are *systems of forces*. External anatomy cannot possibly establish what these organs really are, for it sees only the nutritive matter stuffed into them. And no one can doubt, when he goes more deeply into the matter, that external anatomy sees only the stuffed-in nutritive substances. That which lies at the basis of these organs as force-systems can be seen only by clairvoyant observation. And what we see justifies our nomenclature, because we discover the outer cosmic system duplicated in our inner cosmic system.

We stated yesterday that the organism may develop too strong an inner vital activity. Each separate organ may develop too strong an inner vital activity. This is then manifested in the irregularity with which the organism acts. I indicated yesterday that when, by reason of this excessive inner vital activity, there appears in the inner organs a self-willed life of their own, it is important that something should be set in opposition which will subdue these inner vital activities. That is, when the inner organs transfer too vigorously the external vital activities of the nutritional substances, transform them too much, when they provide an inner product too strongly metamorphosed, we must then set in opposition to them from without something which will dam up, as it were, will subdue the inner vital activities.

How can this be brought about? By introducing into the organism something from the external environment which possesses a vital activity contrary to those of the organs and is capable of combating them. That is, we must endeavour to discover those external vital activities which correspond to the peculiar vital activities of these organs. To contemporary man, who sometimes comes upon such things in the mangled writings of the Middle Ages yet cannot look upon them as anything but a jumble of superstition, it sounds quite amazing when he hears that for thousands of years occult science has not only examined, profoundly and thoroughly, the correspondence between the vital activities of these organs of the inner organic system, and certain external substances possessing the opposite vital activities; but that

also, through countless observations made with the clairvoyant eye, there has resulted the knowledge, for example,
that when the inner "Jupiter" oversteps its limit it can be
checked if confronted with that external vital activity manifest in the metallic substance *tin.* The inner vital activity of
the *gall-bladder,* we combat by what is manifest in the
metallic substance *iron.* And we ought not really to be
surprised to learn that the gall-bladder is the very organ
to be combated by iron. For iron is that metal which we
require particularly in our blood, and which therefore belongs
to the instrument of the ego; and we have seen that in the
gall-bladder we have the very organ which brings about the
connection of the ego with the densest matter deposited in
the human being through the digestive process. In the same
way the *spleen* (Saturn) has its correlative in *lead*; the *heart*
(Sun) in *gold*; Mercury has its own name: that is, the metal
mercury (or *quicksilver*) corresponds with the *lungs*; and
the metal *copper* corresponds with the *kidneys.*

Now, when we introduce into the organism such vital
activities as exist in these metals, in order to combat the
excessive vital activities
of the inner organism,
we must realise that
everything in the organ-
ism is more or less inter-
related with everything
else; and indeed that the
individual organ-systems
were formed in a mutual
parallelism one with the
other. For it is not as if
there first existed in a
finished state what we

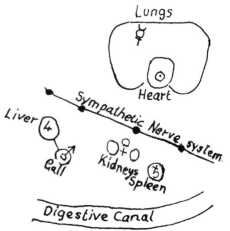

have here merely sketched in our drawing, i.e., what we may call the headless man; but rather the brain and the spinal cord form themselves simultaneously with the other organs, so that the blood-process extending downward extends also upward. And, just as we have pointed out that there are these two circulations of the blood, so we have similarly an upward action of the lymph-system toward the head, and have, therefore, a dim consciousness apportioned also to the upper parts of the organism. This is true because of the fact that what is incorporated above in the upper blood-stream corresponds in a certain way with what we have described as the incorporated lower blood-stream.

From this we now see that certain of these metals to be found on the earth have their respective kinship with the organs or members which we find embedded in the upper blood-organisation. That which, in the lungs for example, opens itself upward into the *larynx,* thus becoming an organ of the higher human organisation, and which otherwise presses down into the gall-bladder as a dim life, acts correspondingly as a Mars- or iron-system in the larynx which contains the upper part of the lungs. These things are, of course, hard to differentiate; but I should like, nevertheless, to point out some of them. In the same way the upper part of our head containing the brain-formation corresponds, as regards its position in the upper course of the blood, to the position of Jupiter-liver (tin) in the lower course of the blood; and tin, or Jupiter; and, in the same way, between the back of the head and lead, or Saturn. And so it is with the organs which may be looked upon as embedded in the upper cosmic system.

We have been able in this way to extend our reflections to that which is incorporated in the circulatory course of man's blood, as having a connection with this, but also as determining it as the organisation of the seven members of the inner cosmic system. And we have been able to take into consideration the connection with the external world as regards both the normal and the abnormal condition of life. In this correspondence between the metals and the inner organs we have a most interesting fact. And if all that which is contained in manifold form in the statements to be found in our books dealing with therapy is ever assembled and compared, not in chaotic manner but systematically, this picture that we have formed will one day, quite of itself, burst into view as a result of the external facts. We can always affirm, when we work creatively in the right way with the help of occult sources, that we can quietly bide our time, that the facts themselves will one day confirm all this for mankind!

When we introduce into the organism the substances of these principal metals—and they are all metals that pass over at a certain temperature into a sort of vapour in which there is active something resembling little smokelike globules—the particular quality of the respective metals acts upon what is in these seven organs. And just as the metallic element acts upon these systems of organs, so anything in the nature of a salt acts upon the blood-system. Only, we must introduce the salty substance into the blood in such a way that it enters from outside, through the air, through air with a saline content, or through a salt bath; or again we can introduce from another direction, through the digestive process, what constitutes salt or builds up salt, so that we are in a position to bring about from two directions this process which results in the formation and depositing of salt.

When you recall what I explained yesterday as the physical effects of the inner processes of soul and spirit, you will understand that everything which meets the processes brought about by these metals as metals, processes which embed themselves in these systems, forming tiny globules, as it were, is what I designated yesterday as the physical effect of the feeling-processes. Thus the dim feeling-processes and the higher feeling-processes are bound up with that which constitutes inner liquefying processes, on the one hand, when it develops the right inner vital activity, but which, on the other side, can be checked if something is introduced from outside, if the appropriate substances which have their external counter-activities embed themselves in these systems from outside.

When, by reason of excessive digestive activity occurring where the nutritional stream is seized by the ether-body, this body develops a too insistent inner vital activity of its own so that it contradicts that from without—when this process of a self-willed inner vital activity gets the upper hand, we can work in opposition to it through the process of introducing salt in so far as salt works as salt. In the case of an intensified inner vital activity of those very processes which go on where the external nutritional substances are seized upon by the ether-body, signifying too intense a taking up, a sucking up of salt out of everything, the process is combated through the external vital activity of salt.

Then we also have processes which occur outside us as processes of combustion or oxydation, when something or other combines with the oxygen in the air. When substances which readily combine with the oxygen in the air are taken into the organism, they radiate their inner activity most extensively throughout the inner organism. Whereas salts act only when introduced into the organism through the digestion or from without into the blood, and hence can get only a limited access to the inner organism; and whereas we can, with metals, work in as far as the inner cosmic system we have, in the external vital activities of the substances that readily unite with the oxygen of the air, something which radiates through the whole organism, even into the blood: something which is capable of radiating through all the systems of organs. We shall thus find it comprehensible that through such processes as develop too strong an inner vital activity in warmth, which is the outward manifestation of the development of the will, we find ourselves inwardly aroused, as it were, in our entire organism. Such is not the case if we direct our attention to those other processes which constitute the organic processes of thought. We feel there that the actions which, in yesterday's lecture, we connected with salt can take place only in certain organs. From this we see how complicated an apparatus the human organism is, and, at the same time, how complicated is its relation to the external world. Moreover, we see that we have now for the first time set the human organisation with its inner vital activities over against a mineral, inorganic Nature which has not yet been given life, into relation with what salts are, what the particular quality of a vaporising metal is, and what readily combustible substances are.

A similar polarity exists between the human organism and what constitutes the vitally active forces in the external plant world. When we use a plant in such a way that it simply gives up some particular substance, which is taken up by us and works in us as lifeless matter the plant-nature in man is left out of account. On the other hand, the plant element can be taken up by the human organism in such a way that it goes on working in its own particular character as plant, that is, the vital activity of the living plant continues to work in man as the same vital activity which in nature works in the plant. In such a case that process which plays between the boundary of physical nutrient substances and the ether-body cannot take place. For the ether-body is akin to the plant; and the plant is "plant" precisely by reason of the fact that it has an ether-body. The plant-nature is simply caught up at the point where the nutritional stream is seized upon by the ether-body, so that whatever of the plant-nature works into the human organism cannot be taken into account so long as it is in the alimentary canal, but only in those organs involved in the processes to which the ether-body already has its relationship and into which the astral nature of man also works. For this reason the external plant-activity begins its work only when it reaches the inner cosmic system and the sympathetic nervous system and, in so far as it is involved with these, also the lymph-system. The plant-nature no longer extends to the point where the human being opens himself, through the blood, to the outer world. The plant-element is fitted to the central, more inward part of the human being; so that whatever may be sought in the plant-nature in the way of vital activities, capable of combating the excessively strong inner vital activities of the functions of our organism, cannot have any effect at all upon whatever belongs to the *material* substance in the seven organs of our inner cosmic system and in the corresponding organs of the head, and which nourishes itself in these organs; it can act only upon whatever pertains to the activities, the *functions* of these organs. When these functions are disturbed, when they act abnormally, without our being able to say that they are over-nourished or under-nourished, then the vital activity of the plant-nature comes into question. Hence, when an excessive activity of the organs is manifest, we can combat this with something taken out of plant-nature but capable of working in only as far as the seven organs, as far as the boundary of the lymph-system and the blood-system.

It is impossible to go further into the combating of irregularities in the human organism, not so much because we should in any case have insufficient time as because it is better for the Anthroposophist to hold aloof from everything which is at present still involved in partisan strife. What we have thus far set forth is not involved in conflicts where there is far too much fanaticism. For at most, people can take it for pure nonsense, in which case it will share the same fate which for many is to be that of Anthroposophy in general: namely, that it has no worth whatever. Anthroposophy would have to keep silent if it wished not to speak about those things which appear nonsensical to people who are not willing at the present time to accept it. But, if it were to proceed further and investigate the effect of the *animal* element upon the human organism, we should very quickly become involved in strife.

One thing, however, you will have perceived: that this human organism is a complicated system of individual organs and instruments which stand at various stages of evolution, these stages differing very greatly among themselves, and which are connected in the greatest possible variety of ways with the organism as a whole. What it is that works into this physical organisation of man, which we see with our eyes and grasp with our hands, in order that the nutritive substances may organise themselves suitably, may be ordered according to the various organs, this cannot be seen with the external eye but it is disclosed to the spiritual eye of the seer. Everything that has displayed itself before us in the human organism we must look upon as *one single system,* wherein appears both what is young and what is old. We have brought out this fact in individual examples, for instance, in the fact that the brain shows itself as an

older organ and the spinal cord as a younger one; and in the
fact that the brain was once a spinal cord and has transformed
itself out of that. Then, too, we have seen that our complicated
digestive system forms, together with the blood-system,
one single system which is old and has been metamorphosed;
whereas in the lymph-system which cannot take up substances from without but can as yet open only inwards to
the material supplied by the inner tissue, we have a younger
system in comparison with the combined digestive and
blood-system, just as we have in the spinal cord an organ
that is younger than the brain. And this, again, is a very
important viewpoint. When we look at our lymph-system
and all that goes with it we have before us something which,
if it were not embedded there as a lymph-system, and did
not remain shut off but opened itself to the more advanced
stage of its evolutionary process, would progress to a digestive
system and blood-system as the spinal cord evolved to the
brain. Thus the digestive-blood-system presents to us a
lymph-system that has been metamorphosed out of the
substances and tissues of the body, substances and tissues
which, as we know, have to be changed in the body before
they can take on the form which they have inside the man;
whereas the lymph-system, as we have it, is employed to
take up the substances that are produced inside. In the
lymph-system and what pertains to it, we have a simpler
digestive system and a simpler system for mediating consciousness. On the other hand, a system more complicated
than the lymph-system, opening not only to the inner but
also to the outer world, is what we have in the metamorphosed
lymph-system, the digestive and glandular systems.

Everything that appears later, during the course of evolution
of any living creature, is laid down beforehand in the germinal
plan. What I have here explained to you as the complicated

human organisation exists potentially in the first germinal cells of the human being as it builds itself up, when once it comes into existence through the process of impregnation. If we retrace the course, so to speak, from this fully-formed man to the germinal plan, we are able to discover that inside this same life-seed or germ complicated systems of organs in miniature, scarcely visible at first, even to microscopic examination, are present, as the very first plan; present in such a way indeed, that the organs even at that time already reveal just how they are related to one another.

Once we observe that the outermost enclosure of the human being is the boundary of the skin which leads us on to the sense-organs embedded therein, and observe also how these sense-organs are organised so as to extend inward to the nervous system, we shall realise that everything present in the outermost boundary of man must have been transformed out of something else, for this is already very complicated in itself. (The brain, for instance, belongs to this system; to imagine a brain which is not first prepared through other organs, and transformed out of these, is impossible.) We must think therefore of the outer sheath of the human being as it appears to-day, as the product of a transformation from those organs which are its groundwork, as having passed through a transformation similar to that of the brain out of the spinal cord, and to the digestive-blood-system with all its accessories, out of the lymph-system.

Now, it is precisely in everything which we have observed as the brain, that we have a transformed spinal cord system. But here again this spinal cord system shows itself to us at the present time in such a way that we can see that it is an organ in a descending evolution, so to speak. In those organs, accordingly, which represent earlier stages, we have organ-systems formed later and at the same time in a descending evolution. This we must apply also to the lymph-system. In that which confronts us in the human being as the lower man, thought of spatially, we have, in the antithesis, lymph-system and digestive-blood-system, something which transforms the lymph-system into the digestive-blood-system. We must understand clearly, to be sure, that the blood-system itself is such a complicated inward-coursing system that it reveals, even in its very configuration, the fact that it is itself the product of a transformation of a still earlier state, the product of a twofold metamorphosis. On the other hand, that which reveals to us that it has gone through its transformation only once, an opening outward, is the alimentary canal. Therefore we can say that were we to transpose the alimentary canal further into the interior of the body we should keep the inner system of organs closed off right up to the activity manifested by the recent lymphatic system, where only those inner products are taken up that are excreted by the tissues.

Thus in the outer boundary of man, the skin-system, we have the metamorphosis of another system; and in the digestive system likewise we can see the transformation of another organ-system where development is in decline today out of which it has developed. According to the whole nature of the organ-systems as they present themselves to us we have to seek, therefore, for their first or primal plan in such a way that we feel everything we see as the germinal design containing the skin- and the sense-organs and nervous system—to be the redisposition of another system which is to-day inside the organism and in a descending evolution, just as the digestive system in its design is a redisposition of another inner system which is now in a descending evolution. Thus we have, at the present time, both an ascending and a descending evolution already indicated in the "life-seed" of man.

And so we may trace the whole human organism back to a scheme or plan where everything in the separate organs is prepared in the germ. And, in fact, we do see in the human germ which comes into existence through the process of impregnation that in the four superimposed germ-layers (the outer germ-layer or exoderm, the inner germ-layer or entoderm, and the outer and inner middle layers or mesoderma) the four principal systems of the human organism are actually already present, pre-modelled in this germinal plan. Furthermore, in accordance with our evolution we shall have to consider the outer germ-layer, which, in contemporary anatomy or physiology is called the skin-sense layer, as the product of a metamorphosis which reveals

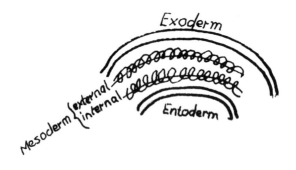

to us its original plan in the outer middle layer. In the outer mesoderm, that is, we have as an embryonic plan in a descending evolution, what appears at a higher stage in the skin-sense-layer; and in the inner middle layer we have in a younger formation and in a downward evolution, what appears in the inner layer or entoderm as the intestinal glandular-layer. When we observe the human germ in its evolution we have in the two *middle* germ-layers, in what external physiology calls the mesoderma, the original plan of the human being still recognisable; whereas the two external germ-layers, exoderm and entoderm, are layers which have undergone a metamorphosis. The two middle layers reveal to us the original state, whereas the two others reveal higher evolutionary stages of this state. And it is only an illusion when external microscopic research does not accurately state the facts of the case.

Now we know that this germinal plan, this life-seed, is formed through the flowing together of two tendencies, the feminine and the masculine, and that the complete germ can only come into being through the living interaction of the two. In both these germinal tendencies, accordingly, there must be included all the processes which, through interaction, form the one single embryonic plan for the complete human organisation.

What does occultism reveal to us regarding the inter-action of the male and the female germs?

It shows us that the female organism, in the conditions of our age, is capable of producing only such a human germ as would be unable, if it were to follow a completely isolated evolution, to develop what we call in its broadest sense the "form-principle." That which leads, therefore, to the final stage of the bony system, thus giving complete firmness to the human being, and which also brings about the final unfolding into a skin-and-sense-system as we have it to-day, could not be supplied through the female. The female contribution is such as to justify one in saying: "What it would bring forth would be too good for this earthly world as it is to-day; for there are not present in our external world all the processes which could serve such an organism, if it were to evolve itself in accordance with the tendency of the female contribution to the whole human organism." It should not be necessary for the human organism derived from the woman to proceed so far as to be of this earth, as we may say, which is the case in the dense deposit of the bony system; it should not be forced to unfold itself in a way that enables it to look out into the present physical world through the senses. On the contrary, it should be enabled to have its inner support in softer material, as it were, than our solid bony system. It ought, furthermore, to be free not to open its eyes so wide toward the outside world, or to open its other senses outward, to the same degree as is the case with the human being of to-day, but to remain more enclosed in its inner life with its perceptions. This represents the female portion of the common human organism: a germinal plan which tends to shoot forward beyond the limit of what is possible in our present earth existence. And this simply because, in the physical conditions of the earth to-day, we have not the requirements essential to so refined an organism, one so little adapted to be of this earth, in the way the bony system is, or to unfold itself outward. Such an organism, under natural conditions, is predestined to death from the very beginning. That is to say: by reason of that which the woman's organism is of itself *unable* to imprint upon the human embryo, this embryo is doomed to death from the beginning.

The other portion which is added to the germinal plan is the male element, and this is in exactly the reversed situation. If the male germ alone were to bring forth the human being, the progress of that organisation which lives its life in an opening of itself outward, as is the case in the skin-sense-system and in the powerful development of what leads to the solidification of the bony system, would overshoot the mark in the opposite direction. The male organisation would be just as little able as the female to create of itself an embryo capable of living. Of itself alone it would just as certainly create a dead embryo as would the female organisation because that which it could create, which it could contribute to the germ-plan, would be so organised, if it were to unfold its forces of itself, that it would have to vanish in view of the conditions actually existing on the earth at the present time; for it would unfold forces which are simply too powerful for such conditions, so that it could not exist as organic life within the confines of this world. That is to say, the male element of the germ does not really come into existence at all; it can act only through co-operation with the female germ. That which stimulates the female germ-plan too intensely, carrying it too far beyond what is possible on the earth, leads the male germ-plan too far downward, below what is possible on the earth. Whatever is destined to death in this female germ, through the excess of those forces which, if they could find any approach at all to the sense-world, would ultimately lead to a breaking up, an inadequacy in meeting the external world, this balances itself with the male germ through the process of impregnation. The forces that are compressed into the male germ-plan, if these were ever to accomplish their growth alone, would lead the whole thing immeasurably below the earthly, would bring the human organisation to a far greater terrestrialising of the bony system, and to an entirely different unfolding of the senses and taking up of the outer world, than is the case to-day. These two organ plans must in their very first beginning blend and come together; for, under earthly conditions, either one of them alone is from the first predestined to death, and only the living interaction of what otherwise gushes over the limits in both directions gives us that human embryo which alone is suited to earthly life.

Thus we see that we have been able, although only in a sketchy way, to comprehend things as far as this point, where the human being is capable of bringing forth his kind. We could go much further by throwing light also upon all the details of the embryonic process. And the more profoundly we should illuminate these, the more we should see that the most minute as well as the most glaring facts, including what has been said here regarding the supersensible force-systems in the germinal plans, prove themselves in the outward expression of these force-systems, in what the human being develops in order that his race may live over all the earth so long as it is going through its present processes.

We have seen at the same time, however, that the earth gives us its densest terrestrialising process, so to speak, in what we call the tendency to the bony system, and its most vitally active process in what we call the human blood-system. And it need be added only very briefly that everything which goes on on the earth in the external physical human organism, in so far as this is visible, forces its way up as it were, into those processes which take place in the blood. And these processes are warmth processes. We have, therefore, in these processes the direct expression of the activity of the blood as the instrument of the ego, of the highest level, that is, of the human organism. Below this are the other processes; uppermost is the warming process, and in this there takes hold, directly, the activity of our soul and our ego. It is for this reason that we feel with regard to so many activities of the soul, what we may call "the transmutation of our soul-activities into a kindling of inner warmth," and this may extend its effects even to a becoming physically warm in the process of the blood. Thus we see how, from out of the soul and spirit by way of the warmth-process, there takes hold down into the organic, into the physiological, what is directed from above. We might show, in connection with many other facts of the external world, how the psychic-spiritual comes into contact in the warmth-process with the physiological, with what occurs behind the physiological. In the warming process, accordingly, we have a transformation of the organic systems in their activities. We find the most manifold transformations in the complicated apparatus of soul and spirit in man; but this physical human organism reaches up as far as the warmth process.

Does this transformation cease at this point? Does that which confronts us as the inheritance of the bony system, proceeding from below upward, extend only thus far, or does heredity continue? Everywhere, below the warmth process, we have transformation; from below upward it reaches as far as the warmth process. What then follows can here only be indicated and then left to the further reflection and feeling of the listeners.

What the organism produces in the way of inner warmth processes in our blood, warmth processes which it conducts to us through all its different processes, and which it finally brings to expression in a flowering of all other processes, penetrates up into the soul and spirit, transforms itself into soul and spirit. And what is it that is most beautiful, the loftiest thing about it, is the fact that, through the forces of the human soul, what is organic can be transformed into what is soul nature! If everything that man can have through the activity of his earthly organism is rightly trans-formed by him after it has become warmth, it then transmutes itself in his soul into what we may call an inner living ex-perience of *compassion,* an interest in all other beings. If we penetrate through all the processes of the human organism, to the highest level of all, to the processes of warmth, we pass as it were through the door of the human physiological processes, above the uppermost heights which are formed by these processes into that world where the warmth of the blood is given its worth in accordance with what the soul has made out of it: in accordance with the living interest of the soul for everything that has being, and its compassion for everything around it. In this way we broaden our life, if our inner life carries us on to a kindling of inner heat, beyond all that is earthly being; we make ourselves one with all earthly being. And we must note the marvellous fact that the whole of Cosmic Being has taken the round about path of first building up our whole organisation, in order finally to give us that warmth which we are called upon to transmute through our ego into living compassion for all beings.

In the Earth's mission, warmth is in the process of being transmuted into compassion.

This is the meaning of the earth process; and it is being fulfilled, since man as a physical organism is embedded in this earth-process, through the fact that all physical processes finally come together in man's organisation as their crown; that everything therein, like a microcosm, in turn, of all earthly processes, opens again into new blossoming. And, as this is transmuted in the human soul, the earth-organism, through man's interest and living compassion for every kind of being, attains to that for which warmth had its intended use in the organism allotted to him as Earth-Man. What we take up in our souls through living interest, which helps us to broaden our inner soul-life more and more, we shall take with us when we shall have gone through many organisations such as enable us to use to the full, for the spirit, everything that the earth could give us as kindling heat, burning warmth, flame of fire! And when, through various incarnations, we shall have taken up into ourselves all that there is of this fervour of warmth, then will the earth have reached its goal, its purpose. Then it will sink beneath us, a great corpse, into indeterminate cosmic space; and there will arise out of this earth-corpse the untied throng of all those earthly human souls who, through their different earthly incarnations, have realised the worth of the outpouring warmth of earth-organisms by transmuting it into living compassion and interest, and into whatever can be built upon these. Just as the individual soul, when the human being passes through the portal of death, rises to a spiritual world and gives over the corpse to the forces of the earth, so to the forces of the cosmos will one day be surrendered the earth's corpse, when it shall have given to us that burning warmth we needed for the compassion which was the foundation-stone of all our higher activities of soul. This corpse which will be given over to the cosmic system, just as the individual human corpse is given over to the earth-system, will be able to see rising above it the sum of all the individual human souls, now one important stage nearer perfection as a result of earth existence, and these will then press onward to new stages of existence, to new cosmic systems. Just as in the earth-system the individual human being, after he has passed through the portal of death, advances to new incarnations, so does the throng of all individual souls, after the earth-corpse has fallen away, advance to new planetary stages of existence.

And so we see that *nothing* in the cosmic system is lost, but that what is given to us in our organism up to the final blossoming of heat is that "material" which, when we have used it up as burning warmth, helps us to find the way to a new and higher stage leading to eternity. Nothing in the world is lost, but what the earth produces, through human souls, is carried over by them into eternity!

Thus does spiritual science also permit us to connect the

physiological processes in the human organism with our *eternal destiny*. And thus will this science, if we view it as something which must so implant itself within us that it is not mere theory or abstract knowledge, fill us with all those forces which show us that we as human beings do not, after all, stand only upon the earth, but in the whole cosmic system! If we learn to think thus about the lofty and eternal destiny of humanity, how man takes the forces of the earth in order that he may work on into eternity, we then receive through spiritual science what must be wrung out of it, not only what we may attain for the sake of knowledge but for our whole man. And if those human beings who divine or already possess this high ideal of knowledge come together in a true brotherhood, harmoniously united in striving toward the highest of all, who understand each other, that is, in their innermost being, this means that there are present on our earth, in its process of becoming, human beings who have the right to be conscious that they bear within themselves seeds which are developing, which can be fruitful for the further evolution of earth and humanity. In all modesty may anthroposophists come together and unite their feelings with what is highest, most universal, in man. And, when men gather in such a spirit, they understand one another in their deepest being; for they acknowledge one another, not merely as individual earth-men and in their earthly destiny, but rather in their eternal destiny.

It was in this spirit that we came together here; and it is in this spirit that we shall go away again, to live in the outside world and perhaps to pass on to others much of what it has been possible to give here as an incentive, even if only in outline, and thus to bring it to new flower. We shall at the same time strive so to work when we are scattered that, although physically separated, we shall be in harmony with one another in living thought, in feeling, and in all our willing. Then shall we be rightly united in that Spirit which ought to be brought to mankind through Anthroposophy. In this Spirit we are about to separate after having been together for a while; in this Spirit we shall remain united in soul; and in this Spirit we shall meet again if it is meant to be.

Complete Edition of the works of Rudolf Steiner in German, published by the Rudolf Steiner Verlag, Dornach, Switzerland, by whom all rights are reserved.

Writings
1. Works written between 1883 and 1925
2. Essays and articles written between 1882 and 1925
3. Letters, drafts, manuscripts, fragments, verses, inscriptions, meditative sayings, etc.

Lectures
1. Public Lectures
2. Lectures to Members of the Anthroposophical Movement and Anthroposophical Society
3. Lectures and Courses on special branches of work:
Art: Eurythmy, Speech and Drama, Music, Visual Arts, History of
   Art
   Education
   Medicine and Therapy
   Science
   Sociology and the Threefold Social Order
   Lectures given to Workmen at the Goetheanum
The total number of lectures amount to some six thousand, shorthand reports of which are available in the case of the great majority.

Reproductions and Sketches
Paintings in water colour, drawings, coloured diagrams, Eurythmy forms, etc.

When the Edition is complete the total number of volumes, each of a considerable size, will amount to several hundreds. A full and detailed Bibliographical Survey, with subjects, dates and places where the lectures were given is available. All the volumes can be obtained from the Rudolf Steiner Verlag, Dornach, Switzerland.